MASTER YOUR MORTGAGE FOR FINANCIAL FREEDOM

NATIONAL BEST SELLER

How to Use The Smith Manoeuvre in Canada to mMake Your Mortgage Tax Deductible and Create Wealth

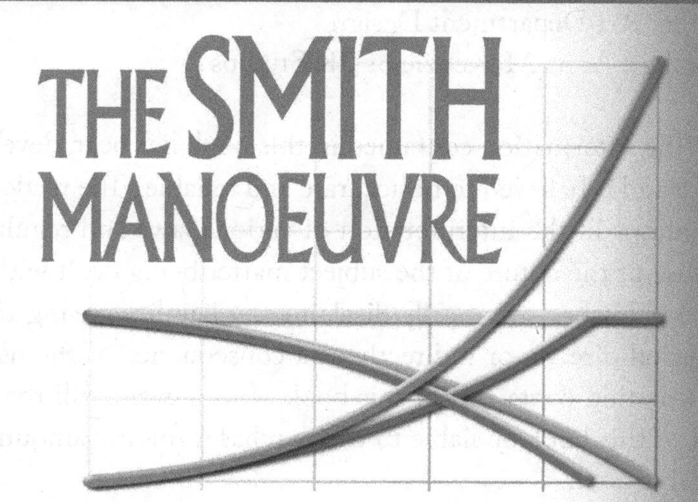

ROBINSON SMITH

www.smithman.net

Published by Smith Consulting Group Ltd., November 2019
ISBN: 9781999171605

Copyright © 2019 by Robinson C Smith
All rights reserved. No part of this publication may be reproduced, stored in or introduced into a retrieval system, or transmitted, in any form, or by any means (electronic, mechanical, photocopying, recording or otherwise) without the prior written permission of the publisher. This book is sold subject to the condition that it shall not, by way of trade or otherwise, be lent, resold, hired out, or otherwise circulated without the publisher's prior consent in any form of binding or cover other than that in which it is published and without a similar condition including this condition being imposed on the subsequent purchaser.

Editor: Danielle Anderson
Typeset: Greg Salisbury
Proofreader: Lee Robinson
Front Cover Design: Art Department Design
Portrait Photographer: Anna McKenzie of BK Studios

DISCLAIMER: The information contained in this book has been developed over several years of experience and is believed to be accurate and reliable. The reader is reminded that there may be variations in the interpretation of various laws and regulations in different jurisdictions because of the nature of the subject matter being dealt with.

The author and publisher specifically disclaim any liability arising from loss, personal or otherwise, incurred directly or indirectly as a consequence of the use and application of any of the information contained in this book. In no event will the author, publisher, or any distributor of this book be liable to the purchaser for any amount greater than the purchase price of this book.

This publication is sold with the understanding that neither the author nor the publisher is engaged in rendering legal, financial planning, investment, accounting, insurance, tax, or other professional assistance or advice. If legal, investment, financial planning, accounting, insurance, tax, or other professional assistance or advice is required, you should seek the services of a competent professional with the required qualifications.

My parents, Fraser and Judy, are the type of people who teach you how to arrange the newspaper, tinder, kindling and logs for a fantastic campfire.

My buddy, Gord, is the type of guy that will do anything to find you a match.

My friend, Aurora, is the type of person who will keep pumping the bellows.

My sister, Jen, is the type of gal who will hide your marshmallows in your sleeping bag.

My long-time assistant and long-time buddy, LuAnn, is the type of friend who won't let anyone with a bucket of water get anywhere near the flames.

My wife, Heidi, is the type of woman who will help you collect wood to keep that fire going forever.

My boys, Digby and Huxley, are why that fire needs to keep burning.

And lastly, to all the hard-working Canadian homeowners and their families looking to improve their financial security...

...this is for all of you.

PRAISE FOR *THE SMITH MANOEUVRE*

"As Chief Executive Officer at the time, I felt it was propitious that Fraser Smith had targeted VanCity to champion his unique financial strategy for mortgage owners in Canada. *The Smith Manoeuvre*, as it was to become known, was simple and elegant. We attracted many new customers over the years by virtue of our support of the program. My question back then still stands today – 'Why isn't every Canadian making their mortgage tax-deductible?' Perhaps the publishing of *The Smith Manoeuvre* will make it happen."

Larry Bell, Chair
B.C. Hydro
Vancouver, B.C.

"Fraser Smith's door ought to have been knocked down hundreds of times. It ought to have been torn from its hinges and thrust aside as mortgage-weary Canadians stormed in to see the man who could help them pay down that mortgage faster and write off the interest like their American cousins."

"Financial Planner Manoeuvres Rules and Banks to Your Benefit"
Andrew Duffy
Times Colonist

"I first read *The Smith Manoeuvre* in my final year of high school. It was the very first finance book I'd been exposed to, and the ideas expressed by Smith gave me a strong foothold for financial security for the rest of my life. After having implemented the strategy for several years I can testify not only to its simplicity, but also to the incredible financial impact that it has on homeowners and especially young families. Not only does *The Smith Manoeuvre* allow us to invest to grow our wealth without any strain on our budget, but it actually increases the amount of Child Tax Benefit that we receive, putting more money in our pockets each month and helping ease the financial burden of raising a family. This book should be mandatory reading for all Canadians!"

Megan Evans
Victoria, B.C.

"I've had [Fraser's] book for about a year and a half now and have put *The Smith Manoeuvre* to work with the help of a financial planner. My husband and I are changed people (financially speaking). Where we were riddled with fear of investment in the past, we are now having a little fun with it while remaining in the 'low to moderate risk' group. We've learned so much and come so far in the past year and a half and our financial situation improved so much that we want to spread the good word to everyone we know."

Anne-Maire Choquette

"I'll keep this short by saying thank you very much for your lifetime achievement of producing a very useful book and sharing it with the public. It has helped my clients tremendously and has created wealth in my own situation as well."

Andre Cyr
Montreal, Quebec

"Just wanted to thank Mr. Smith for caring enough to write such a significant book. I will definitely be implementing his system ASAP. An appreciative mortgage/homeowner."

Rohan Wallen

"I first got introduced to *The Smith Manoeuvre* when a friend mentioned your book to me. I have since read it and found it quite interesting. Being a financial planner, when I first started to read the book I thought there wasn't much new in this UNTIL I got to the part about arranging the mortgage financing. I hadn't heard of any banks arranging this sort of a wrap-around, readvanceable mortgage the way it is described in the book. Innovative!"

Ray Schwalme, CFP, BA
York Financial Group

"Loved your book! Absolutely fabulous! I ordered a copy of your book last week and I read it cover to cover in two evenings. As a former financial planner, I had a sense very early into your book that this would be a life-changing experience for me. I have already called my bank about putting your 'manoeuvre' into action."

Tony Richardson, Project Manager
AdvisorNet Communications Inc.

"Mr. Novak: I recently discovered this wonderful gem of a book which I am sure you are familiar with, *The Smith Manoeuvre* by Fraser Smith. After only reading two-thirds of the book, I am so excited to start the program.... I am contemplating taking a trip to Kelowna just for a consultation with you, to determine if my family and I are in a position to take advantage of the *'Smith Manoeuvre'* plan and get help with implementing as much of the plan as financially possible."

Eric Groom
Airdrie, Alberta

"I would like to tell you that I introduced your strategy to my financial planner and he was very excited about it. He said he'd start to offer this strategy to other clients. Again, thank you for the great idea."

Mark Libant
Ottawa, Ontario

ACKNOWLEDGEMENTS

My debts of gratitude must begin, of course, with my father, Fraser Smith. It is because of him that I even had the opportunity to begin thinking of this latest edition about *The Smith Manoeuvre* – the financial strategy he developed 35 years ago. And to my mother, Judy, who supported him all the way through and offered him the encouragement required to complete a task as large as not only developing a financial strategy for hard-working Canadian taxpayers and making it a success but also throughout the writing of his original book. Dad owes her big time.

Thank you to all the people that have provided their thoughts, advice, encouragement and assistance along the way: *The Smithman Calculator* tech team Ryan Stratton, Alan Harder, Trevor Morrison, Josh Erickson and Charlie Guan; reviewers Denise Clowater, John Gallo, Daron Jennings, John Juhlke, Drew Martin, Gordon McDougall, David Powley and Eric & Jennifer Verscheure; editor Lee Robinson; Julie and Greg Salisbury at Influence Publishing; Rosemarie Bandura of Rose Impressions; Anna McKenzie and Maddy Kirstein at BK Studios; everyone at Holy Cow Inc. for the web and tech support; and strong supporters and advocates, Ivica Sarich, Aurora Winter & Diane Burton, Megan Evans, Jason Henneberry of Tango Financial, Len Shorkey of SMC, Kyle Green of The Green Mortgage Team, and Keaton Kirkwood of Kirkwood & Brennan.

Thanks so much also to Mike Dickson, Francis Rowe and the rest of the gang at Dickson CPAs – they really know their stuff. And a big thank you to Jayne Crooks for keeping LuAnn under control these many, many years.

To my 14-year-old niece, Emily, thank you for providing me with the wonderful illustrations – I know that my readers will love them! And to my 12-year-old niece, Ava, thank you for checking all my math and helping me with some of the big words…

I would also like to give a special thanks to special people acknowledged by my dad in his original book – Larry Bell, Tom Hancock, Preston Manning, Elizabeth Nickson, Herb Grubel and Moshe Milevski.

Most of this book is my own original work but, as this is the acknowledgement section, I would like to fittingly acknowledge that some portions of this book are my father's original writing with minor alterations when I felt it appropriate or when I only needed to update values.

I'd also like to recognize, as dad did, all those dedicated, hard-working Canadian families doing their part to keep Canada a great place to live. It is a privilege to be able to pass on to those families with house mortgages the means to improve their wealth utilizing *The Smith Manoeuvre.*

As dad said in his book, "This book would not likely have been written but for the patience, dedication, loyalty and long and extra hours put in by my long-time assistant and good friend, LuAnn Olson. It's LuAnn who really runs this place, and I'm grateful." I feel I can quote him precisely. She was Fraser's right hand for almost 20 years until the day he passed away and has been mine for 14. She is nothing but magical.

Lastly, to my beautiful wife, Heidi – thank you. You are a force and a wonder.

Robinson Smith

Victoria, B.C.

October 2019

CONTENTS

FOREWORD

So why have I written this book? Well, the passion of my father to fight for the typical Canadian homeowning taxpayer evidently wore off on me. While I have spent the past dozen years meeting with and listening to Canadians explain how they make a decent living but are finding it so hard to progress, my dad, Fraser, did the same for almost 30 years. And one does not tend to spend 30 years doing something they are not passionate about.

So, I joined my father in dedicating my life to developing financial strategies that help lift hard-working Canadians out of the day-to-day struggle of trying to make enough money to be able to take care of their families after the government takes their cut of their income. It's tough trying to support both your loved ones AND a number of governments at various levels…

I have personally helped hundreds of families implement *The Smith Manoeuvre* one at a time, but now it's time to do what I can to reach even more Canadians because, now more than ever, we are on our own. And we need help. All of us.

Throughout the course of this book I will rant a little bit here, rave a little bit there, and at times just generally seem to want to depress you. But that is not the intent – I'm just not good enough a writer to put my anger, discontent or displeasure across in a light which keeps people smiling all the time. But that ain't gonna stop me, because there are answers to many of the problems we face here in Canada, and I'm going to lay them out for you.

Take taxation, for example. Most people try to save money by selling their second car, by turning down the thermostat, by ordering in on a Saturday night because the babysitter raised rates. But one of the most effective ways to improve your net worth and your cash flow is simply by reducing your tax bill. You'll learn how to do that in this book.

Let's look at pensions. Our pensions are not in a solid state of affairs here in Canada and if you are relying on others to provide comfort in your retirement, as many Canadians are, you are incurring significant risk. While many try not to think about it too much because they want to avoid the worry, there is an answer to the pension problem in this book.

And what about mortgage debt? We tend to lose a lot of sleep over this one. But in the following pages you are going to realize that your mortgage can be your friend. No more love/hate relationship for this thing that has given you a safe, comfortable place to live but is sucking your bank account dry. You are going to be thankful you have a mortgage. Actually thankful.

But it is going to require a bit of a mind shift for many readers. The way we have generally been approaching our finances as Canadians tends to lead to the same place – regret. A wish we had done it differently. So, if you think you're on that path that leads to a financial future which won't be as bright as you'd hoped it would be, or if you think you're doing just fine but would like to do even better, open up your mind and read on.

Answers await.

"If you're happy to sit at your desk and not take any risk, you'll be sitting at your desk for the next 20 years."
- David Rubenstein

INTRODUCTION

Dear Reader,

This book can mean the difference between several vacations a year as opposed to only one.

It can mean the difference between both your kids going to university versus neither of them.

It can mean the difference between hardly ever arguing with the love of your life about money or seemingly always.

It can mean the difference between getting in your Winnebago and travelling to Mexico every winter or having to spend every winter in the cold.

It can mean the difference between playing golf three days a week when you're in your 70s or working as a greeter at a big box store.

It can mean the difference between ever-present peace or ever-present concern.

And so, I congratulate you on taking the first (or your next) step on the journey to improved financial security. I congratulate you because it is no secret that many Canadians are reluctant to take control of their life as regards personal finances because a) it can be boring, b) it can be confusing, and c) personal finances have to compete with all the other demands of life. And last but not least, most people simply don't like to think about money and their future because when we look at what it takes to get through the cost of life now, it is difficult to see how we are able to find any more money to improve our future security in the first place. And so we procrastinate.

But procrastination doesn't necessarily stop us from worrying. We Canadians are worried about how we are going to be able to afford to buy a home, about how we are going to be able to pay for it once we have it, about how we are going to be able to support expanding families and the cost of education and summer camp. We are tired and frustrated and angry that we are having to pay more for less and can't afford some of the things we have worked so hard to be able to afford. Arguments about money are having a poor effect on our relationships. Sounds doomy and gloomy, I know, but we are living in times which make it difficult to be as optimistic as we'd like to be...as we used to be.

This Book Is Potentially Worth Hundreds of Thousands of Dollars to You

But I suggest you read on because the value to you and your family from what you will learn in this book can be significant.

The financial benefit to a typical Canadian homeowner who implements *The Smith Manoeuvre* is in the area of around $400,000 over the life of their 25-year mortgage. That is what this book is potentially worth to you.

In fact, that is just the typical base-case scenario – there is a very real chance that your benefit could be much greater. In many cases we see projected improvements in net worth of over a million dollars.

The chart in figure I.1 demonstrates the improvement in net worth when comparing a homeowner paying off their mortgage conventionally versus the 'Plain Jane' *Smith Manoeuvre* and *The Smith Manoeuvre* with only one of the several available accelerators. I would like to first note, however, that in this scenario, and indeed in all the comparative scenarios we'll look at in this book, the house values for any comparison are not included in the net worth or benefit increase calculations. This is because the value of the house will be the same regardless whether the homeowner implements *The Smith Manoeuvre* or not. So the improvements are the actual projected improvement in net worth regardless of house value. Further, any future value projections do not include the effect of taxation as it is impossible to know anyone's given tax situation.

So back to the example at hand – the comparison of no *Smith Manoeuvre*, vs the 'Plain Jane' *Smith Manoeuvre*, vs *The Smith Manoeuvre* with one of the accelerators. Basic assumptions are: annual income of $100,000, marginal tax rate of 38.29%, mortgage balance of $350,000, mortgage rate of 3.5%, secured line of credit rate of 4.45%, portfolio growth rate of 8%:

COMPARATIVE STRATEGY SUMMARIES FOR A TYPICAL CANADIAN FAMILY

	Debt		Tax			Net Worth after 25 Yrs.		
	Start	End	Deductions	Refunds	Time	Investments	Debt	Net Worth
A. Conventional Way	$350,000	0	0	0	25.00 yrs	-	-	-
B. The Smith Manoeuvre Way	$350,000	$350,000	$186,532	$71,423	22.00 yrs	$743,708	$350,000	$393,708
C. The Smith Manoeuvre w/ Cash Flow Diversion	$350,000	$350,000	$250,364	$95,864	15.67 yrs	$1,242,971	$350,000	$892,971

The Plain Jane Smith Manoeuvre (scenario B) generates a net worth improvement of over $390,000 compared to the conventional way (Scenario A). When we add the Cash Flow Diversion Accelerator of $500/month (scenario C), the improvement is over $890,000.

Fig. I.1

We can see a large improvement with just the 'Plain Jane' *Smith Manoeuvre*, but this typical family, were they to implement scenario C of the chart, would enjoy a net worth improvement after 25 years of almost *$900,000*. In addition, instead of taking

25 years to pay off their expensive, non-deductible mortgage debt, it has taken only 15.67 years. A significant improvement.

And any increase in your personal financial security can be achieved with no additional cash outlay from you on a monthly basis. This improvement in your net worth needs *no more money from your pocketbook* than what you are already spending on your existing mortgage and investment program (if you have one). What we are talking about here is a simple, low- or no-cost, one-time restructuring of your personal finances that will enable you to invest significant amounts of money on a monthly basis where no money existed before. The month before you read this book you couldn't afford to put anything away, 30 days after reading this book you are able to put away hundreds, maybe thousands of dollars a month. Each and every month. Again – with *no new money from you required.*

I would like to assure you that the principles in this book are not new. Well-off people, small business and big business have been employing these principles for years and years. What is new, though, is that *The Smith Manoeuvre* allows the average Canadian homeowner to employ the exact same principles that has created wealth for those better-heeled citizens and businesses, whereas before it was financially beyond them. It is not beyond them anymore. It is not beyond you anymore. And even if you are financially better off than the 'average' Canadian, this strategy can help you as well. Are you currently investing for your future already? If so, great, but how would you like to be able to invest even more? Whatever your financial future looks like right now, it can look better.

Today you are going to learn how to re-engineer the way you deal with your house mortgage. When you implement the strategy you are about to discover, you will begin to build an investment portfolio of your own choosing. You will decide whether you want to invest in stocks, bonds, mutual funds, investment real estate, your own business or somebody else's business. These investments will be free-and-clear. It will also cause the taxman to send you annual tax refund cheques, big and growing ones, until you die at a ripe, wrinkly age. The tax refund cheques come every year, they get larger every year, there is no tax on them, and it is all perfectly legal. But that's not all. These tax refunds will enable you to eliminate your big, ugly, expensive mortgage in record time – years ahead of where you would be without this strategy.

See Benefit NOW, Not Later

There are many articles and books written that show you how to pay your mortgage off faster, and this is good because it means you will pay less interest to the bank over the life of the mortgage. But it is important to understand that these strategies, such as switching from monthly mortgage payments to making accelerated payments, are only effective because you are putting *more of your own money* against the mortgage *sooner*. It is the 'sooner' part that shortens the life of the mortgage, thus reducing the total amount of interest that you will pay. While that's good, it is still *your money* that is being *spent sooner*. The sacrifice is that you are spending more of your personal cash flow now and the payoff for you comes at the back-end of the mortgage, which is many years off. Would you like to not have to sacrifice your personal cash flow now? Would you be interested in having your payoff start right now?

Before you adopt the assumption that this is too good to be true, consider that *The Smith Manoeuvre* has been operating continuously since 1984 and tax lawyers from several of Canada's top law firms have confirmed to several large financial institutions that this is a creative but legal financial strategy. *The Smith Manoeuvre* is described (sometimes poorly, unfortunately) in entries on several online financial education websites. Canada Revenue Agency (CRA) auditors actually interviewed my father, Fraser, in his office about *The Smith Manoeuvre* strategy, and walked away satisfied. There are employees of the CRA employing the strategy for themselves on their own homes. The strategy was tested and perfected over a period of almost two decades before Fraser opened it up to the Canadian public by publishing his book in 2002. Since then the book has sold close to 60,000 copies and has helped thousands of Canadian families make their futures brighter.

My father developed *The Smith Manoeuvre* many years ago for a particular reason, and I am putting this book out now for the very same reason: we Canadians do not have it easy. Sure, on the average, the financial life of the average Canadian is, well, average. But you can't trust averages: when you are sitting on a block of ice with a bare ass and your hair is on fire, on the average, you feel okay... Yeah, we have it okay – it's difficult to say with a straight face that we have it 'tough'; after all, we live in a first-world country and have access to much more than the vast majority of our global citizens – but we don't have it *easy*. We are faced with a number of challenges which make it difficult to improve our lot in life, but we *can* have it better.

We *can* enjoy increased wealth, improved physical security, more emotional security, a more comfortable life for our family, and a better (and earlier!) retirement. We *can* be stronger. Both as individual Canadians and Canada as a whole.

All I ask from you, dear Reader, is to have an open mind, a new curiosity, and that you read through this book actively and mindfully. I ask this because whether you decide this strategy is for you or whether you decide it is not, we all need to have a full and rounded understanding before we make a decision. It is by far better to make a decision with all of the information than otherwise.

If you take me up on my challenge, after reading this book I assure you that you'll be one step closer to being better equipped with the knowledge and tools to integrate a results-oriented strategy that is both very legal and very powerful. But you don't have to do it alone – there are trained and accredited *Smith Manoeuvre Certified Professionals* that are able to guide you in the set up and implementation of the strategy and help ensure you stay on track.

There is a team of professionals standing by for you.

Read with Purpose and Intent

This book is designed to give you a solid understanding of *The Smith Manoeuvre* – a financial strategy that will transform your non-deductible mortgage loan into a tax-deductible investment loan which can increase your wealth significantly. This strategy was developed to take you, the Canadian homeowner, from the financial and emotional uncertainty arising from big, never-ending mortgage payments and insufficient retirement savings, to a place where you can find the comfort that accompanies significant, steady and stable long-term financial improvement.

Undertaking any new decision around personal finance requires full understanding of where you are now and where you want to go. I have no idea where you are right now (although I have a pretty good idea if you picked this book up…) but I do know where you want to go. Up. You want to move upwards with regard to improving your net worth, your cash flow, your retirement prospects, your financial stability and also, in a sense, your emotional stability. This book will explain how you can do just that. But it is just the beginning. Too often we pick up a book, read it, and set it aside and forget about it.

Ellen Langer is a Harvard psychology professor and author of at least 11 books. If you simply Google 'Ellen Langer poptech' you will be directed to a YouTube video in which she discusses mindlessness and mindfulness. Now, I understand this may be a strange thing with which to lead off in a book on personal finances, but there is a great deal of relevance, specifically near the beginning of her talk where she defines 'mindlessness' and 'mindfulness'.

"Mindlessness – an *inactive* state of mind characterized by reliance on distinctions, categories drawn in the past:

1. The past over-determines the present
2. Trapped in a single perspective
3. Insensitive to context
4. Rule and routine governed
5. Typically in error but rarely in doubt

Mindfulness – an *active* state of mind characterized by novel distinction-drawing that results in:

1. Being situated in the present
2. Sensitive to context and perspective
3. Rule and routine guided
4. Phenomenological experience of engagement
5. Noticing novelty reveals uncertainty"

I want to bring this to your attention because through the course of reading this book you may well come across a concept or two which go against what you have been taught all your life. But as professor Langer describes in her video, we can have principles or concepts so ingrained from our past that we are reluctant or refuse to accept that there can be a different, new, or updated reality.

Times change, realities change, what once was wisdom or fact becomes wisdom or fact no more – remember when everyone 'knew' the earth was flat? So, I ask that when reading this book, you simply do so with openness and mindfulness.

Read Actively

This is a book on personal finances. And very few things of a practical nature are more important to your present and future well-being as making the right decisions for you and your family, so here are some suggestions:

1. Make a list of goals that are important to you. Do you need more cash flow now? (…and hands go up across the country…) Is your goal to be able to retire sooner

than currently seems possible? (…and hands *stay* up across the country…) Are you afraid you will have to sell your home in retirement or sign up for a reverse mortgage in order to not have to buy ramen noodles in bulk from Costco? (…arms getting tired now…) Did you buy this book in the hopes of improving your sex life? (…most hands go down except for a few who thought *The Smith Manoeuvre* was developed for something else…) In other words, what do you hope to get out of this book?

2. Read with the goal of understanding everything in this book – write in the margins, dog-ear the pages and underline important ideas. You can find some free resources at www.smithman.net which will help you stay on track including checklists, tax tips, basic financial calculators, as well as a link to subscribe to *The Smith Manoeuvre Newsletter* which will give you timely and valuable updates on tax and regulatory changes. There is also a free list of suggested reading you can access on the website to further your financial education.

3. Direct a family member, co-worker or friend to www.smithman.net to get their own copy, lend them yours, or send them to the library so you can discuss the content with someone close to you for more clarity.

4. If there is any part of this book which you don't understand, read it again, and if still no dice, go to smithmanoeuvre.com/info-request and ask me. Only with full information can you make the best choices for yourself. Whether you undertake a certain course of action or decide to reject it, it is best to do so with confidence.

This Book Is Just the Beginning Whether You Are a Homeowner…

Let this be the beginning (or better, the continuation of,) your financial journey. Let it be a spark in your quest to learn deeply about personal finances for the betterment of your future. Books can give you an understanding of a concept or strategy but in order to really embark on a new tack with confidence, you may want to visit our website and look into *The Smith Manoeuvre Homeowner Course*. This will expand on concepts presented in the book and introduce new ones to give you a fully-rounded understanding of the details, intricacies, functionality and processes, myths, common mistakes as well as a detailed explanation on how to get the most out of *The Smithman Calculator* – probably your most important tool in discovering the benefits that *The Smith Manoeuvre* can provide you and your family.

Most people who learn about *The Smith Manoeuvre* are eager to see the potential benefits relating to their unique personal financial situation and specific mortgage details. The problem is it's a complicated calculation. The good news is I have solved this problem for you. I have developed the new and improved *Smithman Calculator* and it will answer your questions within just a few minutes, potentially saving you hundreds of thousands of dollars. If you don't have it already, you can get it at www.smithman.net for around what you would pay a babysitter for a night out. Seems like a reasonable investment.

Lastly, I highly recommend you work with accredited *Smith Manoeuvre Certified Professionals (SMCP)* to make sure you get all the i's dotted and t's crossed in order to take full advantage of your own *Smith Manoeuvre*, which is typically worth around $400,000 or more in net worth improvement – many times much more. It does not cost you any more to work with these certified, trained, vetted and hand-selected *SMCP* professionals. But it could cost you much more if you don't…

…Or a Financial Professional

And if you are a financial professional intent on providing your clients with more – more wealth creation opportunity, more service, and more value – then look into *The Smith Manoeuvre Certified Professional Accreditation Program* to join the increasing number of financial professionals getting accredited, or schedule me to speak to your clients or company staff or agents at smithmanoeuvre.com/info-request.

All of the Canadians looking to implement *The Smith Manoeuvre* are going to need trusted, educated and certified advisors to help guide them along the way. There are too many professionals out there who, despite their best intentions, do not fully understand the strategy. Like anything, a *little* knowledge can be a dangerous thing. But *full* knowledge can be very powerful.

Let's Do This!

My hope is that by reading this book and taking just this one step to learn about personal finances, you will continue to learn going forward, regardless whether you feel this strategy is right for you and regardless whether you are a homeowner or a financial professional. So try to take an interest in your personal finances even outside of this particular strategy.

Get your spouse or partner interested, get your kids interested, your extended family and friends. We all need to educate ourselves further on money and how we can make more of it, keep more of it, and grow more of it; not because we are greedy, but because it makes us stronger. And stronger Canadians make a stronger Canada.

CHAPTER 1

WHAT THE WEALTHY KNOW ABOUT YOUR MORTGAGE THAT YOU MAY NOT

Death Pledge?!

The *definition* of the word 'mortgage':

"A mortgage is a debt instrument, secured by the collateral of specified real estate property, that the borrower is obliged to pay back with a predetermined set of payments. Mortgages are used by individuals and businesses to make large real estate purchases without paying the entire value of the purchase up front. Over a period of many years, the borrower repays the loan, plus interest, until he/she eventually owns the property free-and-clear. Mortgages are also known as 'liens against property' or 'claims on property'. If the borrower stops paying the mortgage, the bank can foreclose." (investopedia.com)

The *origin* of the word 'mortgage':

'mortuus' ('dead' - Latin) —> 'mort' ('dead' old French) + 'gage' ('pledge' old French) = 'Mortgage' ('Dead Pledge' old French) —> 'Mortgage' (late Middle English)

So basically, 'death pledge'. And ain't it apt? Yes…yes it is.

What Does Your Mortgage Actually Cost You?

This is the math that nobody except the bank wants to do. You may have actually worked it out when you got your first or most recent mortgage, but most people don't want to because they know it's scary. Very, very scary. If you don't yet have the comprehensive *Smithman Calculator*, on *The Smith Manoeuvre* website I have a simple free calculator which will quickly let you know how much you will have to earn to pay out the remainder of your mortgage. All you need to know is your current mortgage balance, rate, remaining amortization, and marginal tax rate. It can be found at www.smithman.net, but please – only check it out if you have a strong stomach…

But for now, let us look at a $400,000 mortgage with an interest rate of 4.0%, an amortization of 25 years, and a 40% marginal tax rate for you, the homeowner. What is the cost to you?

Well, first thing that comes to mind is that you need to pay back the original $400,000. That's obvious. And equally obvious is that you need to pay the bank their interest. You are borrowing from them and it comes at a cost that you accept. At an interest rate of 4.0% over 25 years, the total amount of interest you will pay to the bank for the privilege of borrowing that $400,000 is $231,224. So now we're up to $631,224. Ouch. Do you want to stop there? I certainly wish we could, but the fact is that before you have the money in the bank to make that mortgage payment, you first need to pay tax on your income. And over the course of this 25-year mortgage, based on your 40% marginal tax rate, you are going to pay $420,816 in taxes before you can even make those principal-plus-interest mortgage payments. So what's the grand total? How much do you have to earn at your nine-to-five in order to pay off that mortgage? $1,052,040. Over *one million dollars* to pay off that $400,000 loan. That's a lot of hours at the office.

This very thing that got you into a home where you can live and raise a family in peace and serenity, is the very thing that now threatens your peace and serenity. Because of this mortgage you aren't able to put near enough away for your future retirement – if anything at all. When the size of your mortgage payments is tacked on to the taxes you must pay and the bills of life you must cover each month, how is one supposed to even dare think about retirement?

But don't fret. There is a fix.

Debt - The Bad, the Ugly...and the Good

In Canada, when you borrow to buy a car, to go on a vacation, to consolidate your consumer loans or to buy your home, you are prevented by law from claiming the annual interest expense of these loans as a tax deduction. Americans generally can deduct some of this interest at tax time, and accordingly they pay less tax than we Canadians. This is a major factor when trying to figure out why an American lives to a higher standard than his Canadian counterpart.

Sounds like we are doomed. But just a minute – one type of interest in Canada *is* tax-deductible. If the money you borrow is for the purpose of investing, where you can reasonably expect to earn income, then the interest on *that* loan *is* tax-deductible.

Remember this – the test for deductibility of interest is: *What did you do with the money when you borrowed it?* Bought a car? Forget it. Bought a home? No dice. The loan interest in these examples is *not* deductible because the purpose of the borrowing was *not* to invest with the expectation of earning income, it was for consumption.

So we have a problem. You already own a house with a mortgage, which is not tax-deductible. You already have the bad-debt mortgage – is it too late for you?

Not if you know how to utilize *The Smith Manoeuvre.*

What Is *The Smith Manoeuvre*?

The Smith Manoeuvre is a creative, legal financial strategy designed for Canadian homeowners to convert the non-deductible debt of a house mortgage to the deductible debt of an investment loan. This simultaneously ensures the elimination of your non-deductible mortgage in record time while building a free-and-clear non-registered *'Personal Pension Plan'* and enjoying substantial tax refunds each year for years to come. Your mortgage will melt away as fast as your investment portfolio grows.

The wealthy class has used this strategy successfully for years with the blessing of the taxman, and this book extends the knowledge and provides instructions to the rest of us. It can make a huge positive impact on your family's net worth and financial security.

Bad-debt loans, such as car loans, vacation loans and especially home mortgage loans, cost Canadians huge amounts of non-deductible interest every year. If this same amount of interest was a tax deduction, impressive tax refund cheques would start appearing as gifts from the taxman each year.

The Canada Revenue Agency (CRA) will be quite happy to send you a big, juicy refund cheque every year until you die at age 130 or so. You only need to take the time to reorganize the structure of the debt you are already carrying. Then the tax refund cheques start coming.

Just How Large Will These Cheques from the Taxman Be?

The interest on a new $300,000 amortizing mortgage at 5% would be about $13,500 in interest expense in the first year, non-deductible, so no tax refund for you. However, if this mortgage was an interest-only tax-deductible mortgage, and if you were at the 40% marginal tax rate, you would receive a refund cheque from the taxman for $6,000.

If your tax-deductible mortgage were $600,000 at 5%, your refund from the CRA would be double at $12,000. No tax to pay on it either. And these refunds will come year after year. No strings attached.

There Is Another Large Advantage

If you are a Canadian using *The Smith Manoeuvre*, in addition to the gift of generous tax refunds, you will meet another objective common to all of us. You will become the owner of a portfolio of assets such as stocks, bonds, mutual funds or investment real estate. You could invest in your own business or someone else's business. You will choose the investments. The assets will be free-and-clear – they will be unencumbered. The purchase of these new assets will begin *now*, the generation of tax deductions will begin *now*, and the non-deductible mortgage debt will begin to disappear *now*.

The tax refund cheques are great, and to see that ugly mortgage melt away before your eyes is superb. But the integrated benefit of a free-and-clear investment portfolio growing rapidly in your hands is truly magnificent.

What Should You Do?

You already have the mortgage loan, maybe a car loan, or maybe a consumer loan or line of credit, some credit card debt – all non-deductible interest loans. You would be glad to be building an investment portfolio if you could, but you feel you need to get your debt paid off first.

Your plan is to get the debt down over the next several years, and then you expect to be able to start an investment program. Most of the financial planning books tell you to do it that way – pay off your mortgage, and then start an investment program. Your friends, family, neighbours and workmates are all doing it that way, so it must be right. But it's not.

There is a much better way. Organize your financial life to set up *The Smith Manoeuvre*. It is easy and there are knowledgeable professionals waiting to help.

So, in summary, most Canadians would like to:

1. get rid of their house mortgage as soon as possible, and
2. own a significant amount of investments to ensure a financially successful retirement

Most Canadians attack these two goals sequentially, and many financial planners encourage them to do so – first pay off their mortgage, then start an investment program.

What's Wrong with That?

It is better than doing nothing, but to take 25 or 30 years of your life to deal with the mortgage before you begin to invest will lose you 25 or 30 years of compounding time in your investment portfolio.

The Smith Manoeuvre has you getting rid of your expensive, non-deductible mortgage very quickly while *simultaneously* starting your lifelong investment program. We can accomplish these two objectives at the same time, starting *now*. Wealth creation takes time, but *The Smith Manoeuvre* gives you the gift of all the time you have remaining for the rest of your life to build your wealth while getting rid of that bad-debt mortgage quicker than you thought possible.

In addition, new money from the taxman begins to be generated *now*. *Now* is very important. It matters not how old you are, how wealthy you are, or whether you're a socialist or a free-enterpriser. The bad news is that you have the wrong kind of debt, and it's killing you slowly. The good news is that it is easy to remedy.

Remember that old saying, "Today is the first day of the rest of your financial life." You can optimize your financial future by engaging the power of *The Smith Manoeuvre*. Take action *now*...but first let's be clear on *why* we're taking action.

Most of Us Struggle...a Few Don't

What do you want? What is really important to you?

When you think about what would make you happy, remember that this isn't a test. We are all entitled to live our lives the way we want and we are all entitled to set goals for ourselves as we see fit. There is no judgment tied to this question.

Is 'what you want' along the lines of being able to take luxurious vacations or acquire material goods such as shoes, cars or boats? Is the alleviation of personal stress and worry about immediate concerns such as paying bills and the mortgage what you are aiming for? Or maybe more down-the-road concerns like not having to worry about supporting yourself in retirement or where you will be able to afford to live as a senior? Maybe you feel you have things covered for yourself so your goals are more targeted at being able to support others close to you. Perhaps you want to be able to support your church or a charity that is close to your heart. What do you want?

Me? I have most of the above 'wants' on my wish-list, and you probably do too. We're human, so we want the best for ourselves. And we're human, so we also want the best for others.

But here's the problem: I can only afford to acquire so much, or help so much, at any given time. My will and desire may be boundless, but there is always a financial constraint. Some people are faced with less constraint than others, but the fact remains that one extra dollar would always do a bit more, no matter who you are.

> "I love money. I love everything about it. I bought some pretty good stuff. Got me a $300 pair of socks. Got a fur sink. An electric dog polisher. A gasoline powered turtleneck sweater. And, of course, I bought some dumb stuff, too."
>
> **- Steve Martin**

How Do We Get That Extra Dollar?

Okay, so let's get that extra dollar. Easier said than done, many will say – if just *wanting* that extra dollar were enough, everyone would have lots of extra dollars and instead of writing a book on how to create wealth, I'd be writing a book on how to spend it... But there is a way to get that extra dollar, and it is easier than you think. All it takes is a decision, a few weeks or so of financial restructuring, and conviction.

But before we talk about *how* to get that extra dollar, let's talk about *why* you haven't been able to actually get it so far. We need to understand the 'why' before we can get to the 'how'.

It is not fun, fluffy information about unicorns and rainbows, but this information written down on the page will hopefully help inspire you to take the next step toward your financial prosperity, because everyone could use a little inspiration – whether it comes from a place of positivity or not. And it may be this inspiration that will give you that final push to actually say out loud to your partner, your wife, your husband or yourself that you are going to take action. And saying it out loud is the first step.

It's Tough to Get Ahead

But you know this already.

We may live in a decent neighbourhood, drive a decent car, be able to go out for a decent meal every once in a while, but in the background we sometimes have a little trouble getting to sleep, or we wake up way too early in the morning with money on our mind. Or we take a moment when we find ourselves alone to furrow our brow and ask ourselves how we're going to pull off the cost of life.

Of course, there are a good many Canadians who are living comfortable lives who don't have to worry too much, if at all, about how the bills are going to get paid, but the fact is that it is only a small fraction of the total number of Canadians who enjoy that luxury.

The rest of us work hard and long, not because we necessarily love what we do, but because we know that there is life that has to be paid for. I know the old saying, "do what you love and you'll never work a day in your life" but that simply can't be the norm. For a lucky few, yes, but the rest of us sometimes have to take what we can get and to add to the frustration of that, we are *still* continuously struggling to support ourselves, our family and our loved ones. We work hard, we sacrifice, we struggle, we settle, we work hard, we sacrifice… These are the cold, hard facts. So if this describes you, while it may not feel terribly great, at least you can take comfort that you have lots of company.

So why do so many of us struggle but a few of us don't? Why are the wealthy wealthy?

It is because they know something most don't. What did they learn that the rest of the country didn't? Read on, because their lessons can yet be your lessons and you still have time to educate yourself and take action to improve your own personal financial condition.

What the Wealthy Know That You Don't

In calendar year 2017, the world's 500 richest people increased their net worth by $1 trillion. How much of that net worth increase did you see? Exactly. But a bit closer to home, by January 2, 2018, just before lunchtime, the average top-earning Canadian CEO had made as much as the typical Canadian worker did all of 2018. And January 2 was the *first* business day of the year. Think about that – less than half a workday and they raked in as much as we did for the entire year.

Have you ever heard of the Wealth Pyramid? Figure 1.1 is a representation of it.

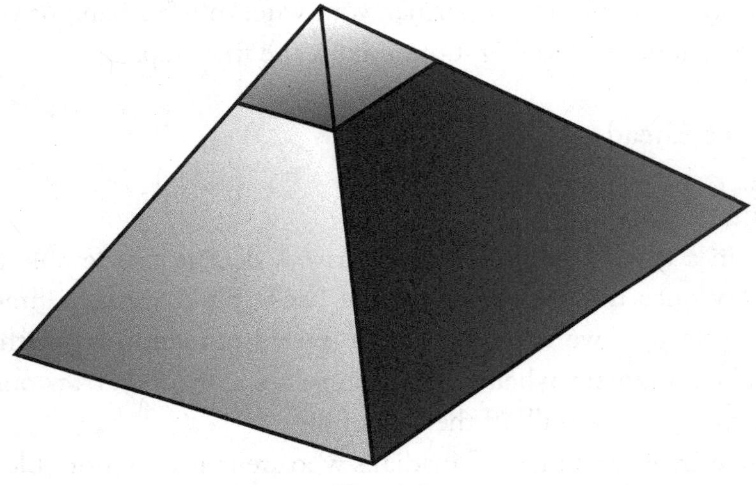

Fig. 1.1

That small section at the tip of it? That is the 'wealthy'. At the top of this pyramid we have the Canadians whose names you hear on TV, read in the paper, hear on the radio. Really wealthy people. Statistics Canada tells us that this 10% of the Canadian population owns over half of Canada's wealth. The bottom 90% of the Wealth Pyramid represents the rest of us – the 'not-wealthy'. We have to share the other half or so of Canada's wealth.

And I'm not saying we're 'poor' – most of us have jobs and families, we're paying off a mortgage on a house we love, we own a car and are able to enjoy a night out every once in a while, but we most certainly would not classify ourselves as 'wealthy'. So we are not wealthy; we do okay…but there's definitely a ways to go on the vertical before we would tell anyone including ourselves we were up there with the ten-percenters.

The wealthy aren't terribly different than the rest of us, but they are not exactly the same as us. How is that? Well, they learned a few things early on in life and they took action.

It really is that simple.

From a young age they looked out at the world around them and saw everybody else structuring their financial affairs exactly the same way. Like a bunch of stampeding lemmings, everybody was scrambling in the same direction on the same path toward the same cliff, thinking that they were doing it the right way, because, well, if everybody else is doing it...

But the soon-to-be-wealthy decided, "No thank you", and went a different way. The path less travelled, if you will. They thought to themselves, "If everybody else is working for a paycheque, struggling to make mortgage payments, car payments, to put gas in the car, braces on the kids and groceries in the fridge, and can barely able to afford two weeks of vacation each year, not to mention retirement, why would I approach my financial life the same way as them? What madness that is!"

The wealthy came to the profound conclusion that just a bi-weekly paycheque was not going to make them rich. I may sound a little glib here with the 'profound' bit, considering as soon as we got our first tiny paycheque at sixteen or so we all likely came to the same conclusion. But we simply were too excited to be saving up for that first car so we could take Betty to the drive-in that we kept at it – kept working for that paycheque – and never really did anything differently throughout our youth and into our adulthood because that's what everybody else was doing and we therefore ended up thinking that was the right way to do it. Inertia. An object in motion tends to stay in motion. A life-work structure in place tends to stay in place.

"I made my money the old-fashioned way. I was very nice to a wealthy relative right before he died."
- Malcolm Forbes

Paycheques Alone Will Not Make You Wealthy

So if the well-heeled understood that a paycheque was not going to do it, what did they discover will? Amongst other things, certainly, but a big one is 'Other People's Money' – OPM. If there are few dollars left over by the end of the month due to life's fiscal demands on our pocketbooks, how are we supposed to be able to save for ourselves; to invest for our retirement?

Well, the good news is that there are plenty of people out there willing to lend us a bit of cash. And the better news is that the Canadian government will even reward us if we use it the right way, that being borrowing to *invest.*

If we borrow to invest with the reasonable expectation of generating income, we can deduct the interest we pay on that borrowed money from our income. This is what we call 'good debt' and it can reduce our tax bill significantly. *Good debt helps us create wealth.* That being said, when we borrow to consume – to buy cars and groceries and gas – we cannot deduct the interest from our income. This is why it is called 'bad debt'. *Bad debt destroys wealth.*

There is a very good reason one is called 'bad debt' just as there's a very good reason the other is called 'good debt'.

Other People's Money

The wealthy got comfortable with debt – the good kind – and you should too.

Many, if not all of you reading this, will know the name Jimmy Pattison. Jimmy is a very successful BC-based businessman and an extremely generous philanthropist. With his natural generosity magnified by his financial successes, Canada is better off for him, no question.

Well, for the past 12 years every day on my way to the office, I have seen good debt – tax-deductible debt – at work and proven very successful. My office is about 20 minutes from my house and every day I pass cars with Jimmy Pattison's name on the license plate surround. I also see billboards with Pattison's logo along the bottom of the structural frame. In fact, I also frequently listen to a few radio stations owned by The Jim Pattison Media Group.

Dollars to donuts, here's what Jimmy *didn't* do to become the success he is: he *didn't* save up enough money to buy his very first car dealership entirely with *cash* and then sit in his corner office waiting for someone to buy a car. Jimmy saved a bit of money for the down payment and borrowed the rest from the bank to buy that first dealership. He used *Other People's Money* – OPM. Then once he had some equity in that first car dealership, he took it out and used it to help finance the purchase of his second car dealership. OPM. Then he pulled the equity out of *that* dealership too to buy another car dealership. OPM. Then again to buy an advertising company. OPM. Then he leveraged the equity in that business to buy a radio station or two.

Do you see? If Jimmy had to save enough dollars to buy his first car dealership in cash, how long would that have taken him? A long, long time. And then how many cars would he have to sell to save up enough to buy his second car dealership entirely with cash? And then his third entirely with cash? Maybe he'd be lucky to have six dealerships by now? But no – he owns around 23 car dealerships representing 12 automotive brands, Canada's largest out-of-home advertising network, 43 radio stations and many, many other companies. Ever shopped at Save-on-Foods? That's Jimmy. Heard of Ripley's Believe It or Not or Guinness World Records? Jimmy and Jimmy.

Jimmy understood that if he borrowed to invest in his business he would not only be able to acquire and build many more businesses than otherwise, but also that he would be able to deduct the interest thus reducing his tax bill. And you can do this too. Maybe not to the extent that Jimmy does (yet…) but the exact same principles that apply to Jimmy also apply to you. *The exact same principles.*

You Behaved like the Wealthy…

So you may be thinking to yourself, "But nobody taught me how to do that. I just didn't know." Well, in fact you already behaved like the wealthy whether you realize it or not. You didn't save $300,000, $500,000 or $700,000 in cash before you bought your first house, right? No, you saved up just enough for a down payment and then borrowed the rest from the bank in the form of a mortgage. OPM. And did that work out well for you? I'm guessing it did.

You borrowed money from somebody else because if you didn't, you'd never have enough to buy the home in which you are raising or have raised a family. You acted, just for a moment, like the wealthy do, and likely have seen your 'investment' – your home – increase in value. Not bad. And hundreds of thousands of other Canadians also acted like the wealthy when they bought their homes.

The only the difference is, they didn't see using *Other People's Money* as an 'investment strategy'. They saw it as a way to buy a structure with a roof that they could live in well before they would be able to if they had to save up the cash for it. They likely didn't realize or connect the dots as to how the structure of that particular financial transaction could translate over to the rest of their financial lives. It's not their fault, it's just that they weren't taught – how are we supposed to know if nobody tells us…?

…And Then You Stopped Behaving like the Wealthy

So for a brief moment, hundreds of thousands of non-wealthy Canadians joined the ranks of the wealthy as regards employing a financial technique that could increase their wealth, but then almost right away, as soon as they got the keys to their new house, they stopped acting like the wealthy and got back on the well-worn lemming path with the rest of Canada's non-wealthy when they committed to their banker, their spouse and their God to reducing their debt at the expense of investing for their future. Why? Because ever since they were young, people close to them have been telling them that "Debt is bad! Don't ever get any debt but if you have to, pay it off as soon as you can and don't get any more!" Maybe it was an aunt, a granddad, one or both parents? But they never heard from anyone that there is more than one type of debt. They simply were not taught either.

Since we have always been told only about the evils of debt, we have avoided it (or tried to avoid it) *except when we bought our house.* Then we couldn't get enough of it. We went for as much debt as a drunken banker would offer us. (I know I did!) But whether we understood/understand the distinction between the two types of debt or not, that mortgage is the *wrong kind* of debt and we rightly know that we want to get rid of it as fast as we can. And we should. Because our mortgage debt, regardless of the fact that it allowed us to buy our wonderful house, is 'bad debt'.

But don't let the simple word 'debt' make you shy away from further employing the techniques of the wealthy. Embrace it. Debt allowed you to buy the asset that, while housing your family, has increased in value over the years and increased your net worth. That fact that bad debt has actually been a good move is, in this case, a unique circumstance. But it is still bad debt – it is not tax-deductible. Good debt – more accurately in our case, converting that bad debt into good debt – can help increase your net worth even more. Significantly.

There Is Such a Thing as Too Little Debt

You've likely been downtown Toronto or Vancouver or Calgary. You've seen the skyscrapers with the company logo in bright lights way up on the top of the building – a telecom company, a bank, a tech company, energy company, manufacturing company… Did you know they have whole floors of that corporate headquarters dedicated to making sure the company has *enough* debt? They are running their models and crunching the numbers and Alex in Accounting on the 36th floor is actually calling up to the corner office on the 55th floor telling Sam the CEO, "Sam, we don't have enough debt today, we need more debt."

But there is bad debt and there is good debt, and that is a very, very important distinction.

Wealthy People Have Mortgages? *Really?*

Wealthy people are just as likely as you are to have a 'mortgage' on their home. The difference is that the monthly interest portion of their 'mortgage' is tax-deductible, and yours is not.

We can learn much from the wealthy. First, as mentioned above, they use OPM – Other People's Money – to increase their own wealth. Secondly, any debt they do take on generates big tax deductions because they only borrow to *invest*. Remember, the test for tax deductibility is "what did you do with the money when you borrowed it?" Borrow to invest with a reasonable expectation of generating income and you can deduct the interest. Wealthy people borrow money like everybody else, but they use it to buy investments such as real estate, mutual funds, stocks and bonds. They will also borrow to buy a piece of somebody else's business, or to put into their own business.

We're Doing It Backwards, Folks

There is a pattern emerging here. Wealthy people intentionally pay for houses, cars, and vacations with their *after-tax cash*. The not-so-wealthy, which is 90% of us, *borrow* the money to buy our houses, cars and vacations. We do it backwards. At great expense to our future net worth and our future financial well-being.

And in any event, when you are paying as much as half of your income in taxes of many kinds, and when you are paying those huge amounts of interest to the bank for your mortgage every month, most Canadians find it very difficult to consider the purchase of investments. So you wait for a better time, such as when the mortgage is retired. Many, many years down the road.

This really hurts your chances of improving your future net worth at a decent rate because the time-value of owning investments dictates that the sooner you own them, the more they will compound their value as the years go by. We need a program that allows us to get rid of our non-deductible house mortgage as fast as possible while *simultaneously* enabling us to be building an investment portfolio as fast as possible. We non-wealthy Canadians generally believe we have to wait until the mortgage is gone before we start investing, and that is terribly expensive.

Let's Quantify

The wealthy Canadian example, let's call her Rebecca, may start with a non-deductible loan to buy her house, just like you. But very quickly, her highly-paid accountants and lawyers show her one of the tricks of the trade – how to convert the bad-interest mortgage loan to a good-interest investment loan.

Example: Rebecca may have a new house with a new and non-deductible mortgage of $600,000, just like you. Assume she also has $600,000 worth of mutual funds she has gathered over the years. Rebecca's tax accountant will be quick to suggest that his client sell her mutual funds, and with the $600,000 cheque she receives, Rebecca will pay off her brand-new mortgage today.

Tomorrow, she will go back to the banker, borrow back $600,000 using the house as collateral, and she will use the borrowed money to buy back $600,000 worth of mutual funds. Rebecca still has her house, her $600,000 in mutual funds and a $600,000 loan, but one important thing is different. Because she borrowed to invest, she has just converted $600,000 of debt from bad debt (non-deductible interest) to good debt (deductible interest). Rebecca may have some taxes to pay on the sale of the mutual funds, and she may have some commissions to pay for the sale and repurchase of her mutual funds, but these costs are small spuds compared to the huge tax deductions she will be getting every year for the rest of her life.

At 5% interest, Rebecca will have a $30,000 tax deduction this year, next year, and every year of her long life that she has the loan. You won't. Unless you decide to learn how to do *The Smith Manoeuvre*.

Wealthy people tend not to pay off deductible loans. Why would they? At the 50% marginal tax rate, the tax department will be sending our wealthy example a cheque for $15,000, tax-free. Every year. You, however, won't get a cheque, *even though you both paid the same amount of interest on your loans*. The cheque from the tax department is significant. There is no tax on it. You can do anything you want with it. It is legal. In fact, it is encouraged.

You are paying the interest as part of your monthly mortgage payment every month anyway. Why not make it tax-deductible? Embrace *The Smith Manoeuvre*, and you will.

The Rich Get Richer...

It doesn't seem too fair, but rather than whimper, let's learn from the wealthy and do our best to emulate their methods. In our example above, the debt conversion was done in one day, but there is nothing to prevent persons of more modest means from accomplishing the same results over a longer period of time, by the month.

There are traps to fall into and rules of order to follow, so do yourself a favour and retain the services of accredited *Smith Manoeuvre Certified Professional* advisors to ensure you optimize your opportunity. For instance, there are rules surrounding selling securities one day then repurchasing the identical securities within 30 days. If you set your borrowing facilities up in the wrong manner, you could foul up your claim for deductibility as far as the tax department is concerned. It can hurt you to try and do this by yourself. Attempting your own financial planning in these modern times is as dangerous to your health as is taking out your own appendix or extracting your own molar. Find professional advisors, ones with a designation after his or her name. These are registered and certified professionals who take courses and pass exams. They adhere to a code of ethics. This would be a bad juncture in your life to try to do it yourself.

...Due to the Magic of Compound Growth

You have the ability to immediately put your mortgage and home equity to work for your advantage. And many will agree that it makes great financial sense to put a dollar to work now rather than later so that you get to enjoy the magic of compound growth.

True story: someone once asked Albert Einstein what he thought was the 8th Wonder of the World. He replied, "Compound growth. No, wait, *The Smith Manoeuvre*...no, hold on, uhh, geez...compound growth, final answer!"

Simply put, compound growth is the growth that one enjoys from the growth on the growth of their investment.

If I invest zero dollars each and every month, religiously, at 8% growth for 25 years, how much will I have at the end of 25 years? Now I know that not everyone reading this is a mathematician who has the powerful and specialized computing programs at their disposal with which to do this calculation, so I'll just tell you. Nothing. Surprised? I knew you wouldn't be.

Now consider this: if I put $1,000 under my mattress each and every month at 0% growth, religiously, for 25 years, how much will I have? I'll have $300,000. That's better, eh?

Now what if I put $1,000 cash each and every month, religiously, into an investment that does 8% per year for 25 years? At the end of it all I would have $951,026. Now we're talking. We're starting to get into some serious retirement comfort. But just a second, you don't have $1,000 a month that you can put aside to invest because life is just too expensive, so that calculation is irrelevant as far as you're concerned. Well, it just so happens that you are one of the many Canadians who have a mortgage. If you employ *The Smith Manoeuvre* you may, in fact, have this $1,000 or so each month.

At this point some of you may be saying that you already have the means to invest $1,000 per month from personal cash each month and so are already on your way to that $951,026 asset value without implementing *The Smith Manoeuvre*. To that I say, fantastic! You are one of the few in Canada that can afford to put something away, meaningful amounts actually, on a monthly basis. But what I also say to that is if that is indeed the case, after 25 years, if you implemented *The Smith Manoeuvre* under these same assumptions, you would have $1,902,052 saved up because you now have $2,000 per month to put to work for yourself (and actually, it would be quite a bit more due to the deductibility of interest but let's just leave it there for now).

Compound Growth Is Powerful

Chances are you have heard this one, but if you take a penny and double it every day for a month (31 days), what would you end up with? I'll save you the math – the answer is over $10.7 million dollars. Starting with one penny. Now that is obviously exaggerating the benefit we can reasonably expect from compound growth in our own investments, but it does demonstrate the power. So put that power to work for yourself.

Picture a snowball growing in size as it rolls down a snowy hill and you are envisioning compound growth. All you did was pack the snowball, set it on a specific course, and let it do its thing. And it's the same with money. Get a few bucks together, invest wisely, and watch the value increase as your earnings are reinvested and earn a return themselves. You are enjoying a return on the original investment and also a return on the return. The longer you remain invested, the greater the opportunity for growth, and this growth accelerates. There is a simple, free compound growth calculator at www.smithman.net where you can input assumptions regarding investment contributions and growth rates to see how powerful compound growth can be.

You can implement *The Smith Manoeuvre* with no new money from your pockets and no new borrowing and can generate significant wealth for you and your family.

Start investing NOW, when you are unequivocally as young as you are ever going to be. Start now and put that power to work for you, not the banks. Do not wait until you've paid off your mortgage to start investing for your future; for your family's future. Procrastinating is expensive. It is terribly costly.

The Objective of *The Smith Manoeuvre*

The debt of the wealthy generates deductible interest to reduce their tax, which increases their cash flow. They get richer. Your debt, your mortgage, is paid for with your after-tax dollars, and generates no deductible interest. The task at hand is to learn how to do what the wealthy do – convert the mortgage loan from bad debt where the interest is non-deductible, to good debt where the interest is tax-deductible. By doing so you will be able to enjoy the wonder of compound growth and watch your net worth increase exponentially.

> "It's not how much money you make, but how much money you keep, how hard it works for you, and how many generations you keep it for."
> **- Robert Kiyosaki**

CHAPTER 2

IT'S TOUGH OUT THERE. ARE WE ON THE RIGHT TRACK?

There is a rumour that the tax department is planning a new tax return for Canadians. The Canada Revenue Agency (CRA) has been listening to citizens who think its format should be much simpler. Now please keep this under your hat as we had to go through some shady backchannels to get a classified copy of the first draft of the upcoming simplified return, but here it is:

Dear Taxpayer,

a. How much did you make last year?
b. Send it in.

Thank you,
- CRA

Anyone reading this book right now who enjoys paying taxes, raise your hand…

...I guarantee you no one raised their hand just now, and I can guarantee that quite confidently because a) you may well be the only one reading this right now, and b) I know you didn't raise your hand.

While we may not actually *enjoy* paying taxes, sometimes we don't *mind* paying taxes. We all understand to varying degrees that taxes are necessary in order for the government to be able to fund social programs, construct hospitals and schools, pave roads, build bridges and keep the streetlamps on at night. And frankly, in an ideal world we should all be *happy* to pay taxes – but that is because in an ideal world our money would be spent wisely. *Our* money.

But where understanding gives way to frustration is when we see our government spend our money in ways that are wasteful. It is often as if the government has no sense of ownership of the funds in their bank account. And honestly, is it so hard to understand why they don't treat that money as if it were theirs? It's because it's not. You earned it and then they took it. Free money! So why should they be careful about how they spend it?

The various governments have been so spurious in the handling of public money for so many years and generations that we, the taxpaying public, have grown used to its mismanagement. Heck, we even expect it. Sometimes we even laugh at it because it is so ridiculous.

Now at this point I want to clarify that I don't necessarily think that all governments are the taxpayers' enemy. It is indeed a very big and difficult task to run a country, after all. I do, however, think that many governments are inefficient, and this inefficiency shows in the way our tax dollars are spent.

How Much Tax Do We Canadians Actually Pay?

Wikipedia maintains a list of personal income tax rankings for as many of the world's countries as possible. At the time of writing, only one country had higher personal income tax rates than Canada. And the Wikipedia list is 260 countries strong. According to this list, we Canadians are the second-highest taxpaying citizenry on the planet. Anyone heard of Tax Freedom Day? The Fraser Institute publishes Tax Freedom Day on an annual basis, and it measures the total yearly tax burden imposed on Canadian families by all levels of government. For 2019, Tax Freedom Day was June 14, meaning that if you had to pay all your taxes up front, every dollar you earned from January 1 until June 13 would go straight to the government.

Sidebar - my dad, Fraser, was fond of telling anyone who would listen, *"Many people think that The Fraser Institute was named after me but that's not the case. The Fraser Institute was named after the Fraser River…which* was *named after me…"* He was a humble man…

Figure 2.1 indicates the highest Canadian tax rates for 2019 (federal and provincial) broken down by province.

HIGHEST CANADIAN TAX RATES FOR 2019
PROVINCIAL AND FEDERAL

Province	Provincial Rate	Federal Rate	Total
Newfoundland & Labrador	18.30%	33.00%	**51.30%**
Prince Edward Island	16.70%	33.00%	**49.70%**
Nova Scotia	21.00%	33.00%	**54.00%**
New Brunswick	20.30%	33.00%	**53.30%**
Quebec	27.56%	25.75%	**53.31%**
Ontario	13.16%	33.00%	**46.16%**
Manitoba	17.40%	33.00%	**50.40%**
Saskatchewan	17.40%	33.00%	**50.40%**
Alberta	15.00%	33.00%	**48.00%**
British Columbia	16.80%	33.00%	**49.80%**
Yukon	15.00%	33.00%	**48.00%**
Northwest Territories	14.05%	33.00%	**47.05%**
Nunavut	11.50%	33.00%	**44.50%**

Fig 2.1

And if you look at those tax rates, it takes no great amount of mathematical creativity to understand that a whole whack of our total household cash is going toward one item. The Fraser Institute, again, calculates that over 44% of the average Canadian's income goes to taxes. Recently I've seen that figure quoted as closer to 50%. If we think about all the other things in life that we have to pay for out of the remaining 50-56% of our income, we realize that we have a relatively small piece of the cash pie remaining to take care of every other expense we run into in life. In fact, Canadians pay more in taxes – federal, provincial, municipal and indirect – than we do on food, clothing and shelter combined. Before we can pay for the basic necessities of life required to *simply continue living*, we must first pay the government a sum more than the total expense of these three life-sustaining absolute necessities.

Figure 2.2 is a diagram of Maslow's well-known Hierarchy of Needs.

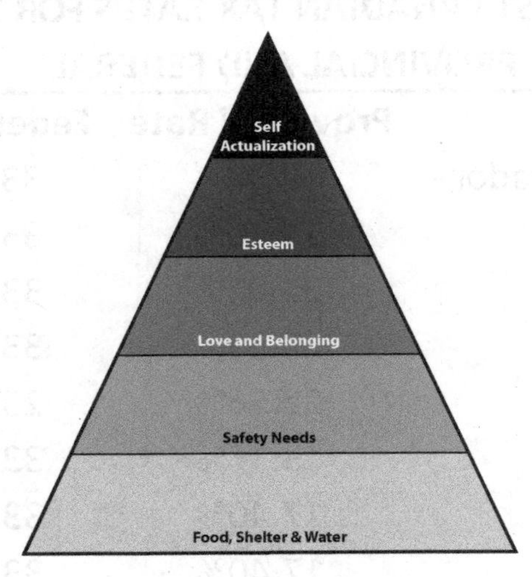

Fig 2.2

However, I suggest that it be modified as per figure 2.3 to reflect the reality we Canadians face considering how the government sees it...

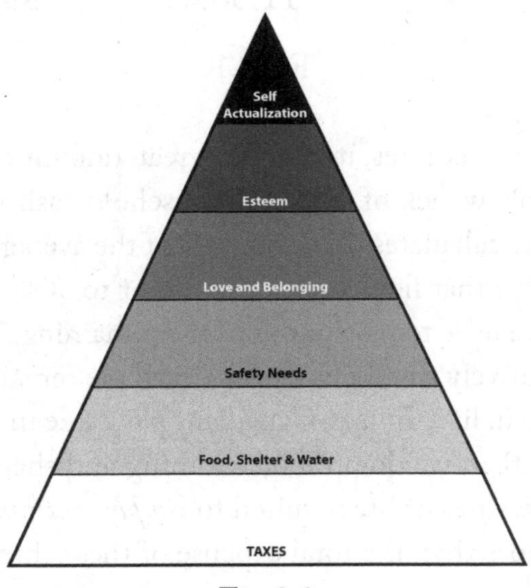

Fig 2.3

"I have never understood why it is 'greed' to want to keep the money you've earned, but not greed to want to take somebody else's money."
Dr. Thomas Sowell

Boiling Frogs

Do you know what we Canadians are? Boiling frogs. You may have heard of the old myth that if you put a frog in a pot of cool water on the stove and turn the heat up, the frog will continue to get used to the gradually increasing temperature and will not try to jump out. It will eventually boil to death. That's us.

We begin our young working lives and start to pay taxes but don't think much of it because we already 'knew' there was such a thing as *tax* and we were already expecting to pay it: 28 degrees in the pot. Then after a while of seeing taxes automatically come off our paycheques we start to complain to our co-workers about *this* tax going up. But we pay it: 37 degrees. We moan about *that* tax increasing but we suck it up and shell it out: 74 degrees. Hooray, *that* tax actually just went down – 68 degrees – but *those* three went up: 97 degrees and we fork it over. And on it goes. We Canadians are taxed higher than almost everyone else on the planet and it doesn't seem there is any relief in sight.

Taxation is one of the major impediments to the accrual of assets for Canadians. It is an immense preventer of wealth creation. It can be a hugely powerful tool for improving quality of life, but have we as Canadians witnessed that to any proportionate degree compared to how much we are taxed? Or have we watched our tax dollars too often squandered at our family's expense with little reward other than for a select few?

Well, What Can I Do About It?

If, as a citizen, I can't successfully reduce the number of taxes I pay or the rates on these taxes, what is one to do? If we as taxpayers are successful in voting out one wasteful government just to vote in another, how do we stand a chance? But if you think there isn't anything you can do about it, think again.

The taxes may keep biting harder and harder but you have the ability to lessen the hurt, because while you may not be able to do much about *tax rates*, there most definitely is something you can do about *how much tax you pay* given *those tax rates*. Let's make the government send back some of the tax that we have already paid them throughout the course of the year when they have taken it straight off our paycheque every two weeks.

Many financial advisors will tell you that one of the most efficient and effective ways to increase your net worth is to simply reduce your tax bill and that's what we as Canadian homeowners have a unique opportunity to do. All shall be explained in more detail subsequently, but first let's have a look at more scary stuff because I'm having such a good time here.

"It takes as much energy to wish as it does to plan."
- Eleanor Roosevelt

The Problem with Pensions

Do you have a retirement plan yet? It's quite possible that you don't. And if this is the case you are not alone. Many people don't. We are busy people trying to just stay on top of the bills that keep filling the mailbox on a monthly basis and the odd expense that we didn't see coming.

Usually we can hold the credit card bill to a reliable balance on a monthly basis but every once in a while something punches us right in the throat and there goes our monthly budget down the storm drain. And so, we understandably tend to concern ourselves with life's more immediate fiscal concerns – making sure we get the mortgage paid, keeping the lights on, car gassed and the children fed, and we find ourselves not thinking about down-the-road issues such as retirement. For one thing, it's unreasonable to really spend too much time on that considering there's nothing we can afford to really do about it now anyways, and for another, it's a scary subject. So we have no plan.

What we do have is blind hope and a vague idea. The blind hope is that there is some sort of pension plan we are able to get on at some point. Maybe we don't have one now but there's always tomorrow, a new job with a plan, whatever the case may be. The vague idea is that we have a house that we can always fall back on in 10, 25, 40 years or so. How exactly will we fall back on it? 'Don't know yet,' we say, 'that's a ways down the road...'

Well, I'll talk about *eventually* using the house to finance your retirement a bit later (see 'Reverse Mortgage') but let's talk about the state of Canadian pensions at this point.

I guess the best way to start this conversation is by asking...

"What Pension!?"

It is a very small percentage of Canadians who are destined to retire independently wealthy; in other words, with the means to take care of themselves without having to rely on friends, family or government. There are reasons for the fact that it is only a small percentage. Firstly, as I mention in this book several times, we Canadians are simply not exposed to any financial education or training of significance. We are not taught how to make more money, keep what we've got, or invest what we have. The odds are stacked against us from the outset, folks.

Another is that our pension system in Canada is inequitable. I'm not necessarily talking about CPP or OAS or other socially-funded income assistance; I'm talking about the fact that your neighbour to the right of you works for the federal government and his wife works for the police service and they both have generous pensions offered by their employers. Your best friend works for a big multinational and has a matching RRSP program. You work for a small independent company and get a wage or salary and that's it. There is nothing waiting for you when you hit a designated age; no cash flow you can expect. Your spouse owns a small home-based business and the only 'pension' for him/her is what they are able to put aside after, it turns out, paying their employees more than themselves once you break it all down on an hourly basis.

So there are many of us who have no choice but to take care of ourselves, and yet we are not. We are not paying ourselves first because not only can we not afford to, but we haven't been indoctrinated into the ways of retirement planning at an early enough age or at all. We have no pension.

"At Least I Have a Pension, so I'm Safe…"

If you do have a corporate pension plan, you are in the minority. One of those few lucky Canadians whom the company is going to take care of in their future retirement to some extent.

Sears.

That should be all it takes to make the lucky minority a wee bit nervous. Airline pension plans? - Mmmm... Wait, what about the university for which I've been working for the past 22 years? - well, just this past year a major Ontario university tried to change the terms of their employee pension plan to their employees' detriment, and they won't be the last to give it a shot.

Do. Not. Bank. On. Your. Pension. Plan.

A bit dramatic, I know, but not without warrant, I assure you.

Sears went under in 2017 and not to mention the 18,000 loyal employees who unfortunately lost their jobs, there were about 16,000 Sears retirees who saw their pension fund shrink by around $250 million dollars pretty much overnight. The executives came out all right – remember those top-earning Canadian CEOs who earned as much in half a day as you did all year?

In fact, a study by the Canadian Centre for Policy Initiatives released in 2019 found that of the 90 TSX Composite Index-listed companies that had defined benefit pension plans for their employees, only a few had fully funded their workers' pension plans in 2017. Collectively, these 90 companies were underfunded by a total of $12 billion, whereas the dividends paid out to shareholders totaled $66 billion. They could have fully funded their plans five times over. But they chose not to.

Is what happened to Sears going to happen to your company? You may think not because your company has not been in the news about any troubles, but the last thing a company wants to have is its troubles advertised, and they will go to great lengths to make sure that when it hits the fan, the public and employees are the last to know. And once it's gone, it's gone. Do not put all your eggs in one basket – diversify your retirement savings and start building *your own 'Personal Pension Plan'* right now. Don't wait.

And the Canada Pension Plan – when things get a little thin on the asset side, all the government has to do is increase payroll taxes. The cost of this is borne by you, whether you are an employer or an employee. In fact, Canadian workers are having their mandatory contributions to CPP increased step-by-step over seven years.

And what could the effect of this be? It has been predicted, quite reasonably, that as workers will have to put more aside in a mandatory savings plan, they will necessarily reduce voluntary savings plans which have historically had a tendency to be invested within Canada. So because Canadians will be investing less in Canada, we will see less investment and growth and expansion in our domestic economy resulting in reduced productivity and job and wage growth. And if we look at the population curve, we have an increasing number of retirees that must be supported by a smaller number of people currently in the workforce. Not a great recipe for a solid pension system.

Lastly, the next time you are in Costco, Walmart or a fast food restaurant, take a good look around. If you haven't already, you will notice many seniors acting as 'greeters' or asking if "you want fries with that?" Do these seniors want to be working there? I would suggest, for most of them, no. I would suggest they would rather be playing golf, Texas hold 'em, tending their garden, casting for trout…anything else. But they have no choice but to work in their 'golden years'.

[Your Name Here] Incorporated

Here's the thing: You are not a corporation. You are an engineer or a bus driver or a school teacher or a marketing manager or administrative assistant, small-business owner, government worker, arborist, plumber, ambulance driver, pilot, cop, [insert here]... But you are *not* a corporation.

And because you are not a corporation, you think and operate differently. You do your best to provide for your family, you do your best to be polite to strangers, to help an old man across the street, to make sure your neighbour's mail doesn't stack up when they go on a vacation. And that is definitively NOT the definition of a corporation.

If I were to ask you, "What is the primary concern of a corporation?" no doubt after consideration you would answer something to the effect that it is to provide value for the corporation's shareholders. And yes, that has a certain nobility and reasonableness in it: If I invest in a company – my hard-earned dollars – and in doing so help this company grow and prosper, then I have helped feed the economy and have created jobs for other people while hopefully making a buck or two in the process. I am risking my money as a shareholder and therefore I should get reward in exchange for the risk.

Why We Don't Trust Corporations…

But here's where it starts to go pear-shaped. It is when the board of directors and managers, when the people in charge of making decisions for the company, start making decisions that, in the righteous vein of increasing the wealth of their shareholders – themselves some of the biggest shareholders, of course – begin to slide into the grey area. We hear about it every day. Big corporations – some of the most 'trusted' corporations in our country – are constantly in the news about questionable sales practices, product recall cover-ups, tied-selling, etc. These are the kind of stories that have left a bad taste in our mouths.

How many times have we seen or heard, "These sales practices [that were caught on tape] do not reflect our corporate policies and we will be conducting a full investigation to ensure this does not happen again"? We need to watch our own backs and that means taking the time to educate ourselves and making smart decisions, expressing our displeasure where warranted, and demanding change because the big banks and corporations *do not* have our backs. As long as our guard is down, they have the opportunity to take advantage of us. So, be alert.

The world needs more lerts.

That all being said, these corporations *do* know how to make money and improve their net worth. They are good at it. Very, very good at it. So let's take a lesson from them.

My point is, we may not, as a provider for our family, tend to 'think' like a corporation (which may be a good thing in many instances), but, to the extent that corporations make money and increase wealth, we can do that too. We have the choice of leaving the grotty bits out but we do have the opportunity to think like those who are good at generating wealth and therefore generate it for ourselves.

We Can Think like the Corporations Where It Helps Us

We can be our family's Chief Financial Officer – the CFO. We can educate ourselves about money, about debt, about wealth accumulation and about risk management. Think about it, while the CFO's office is not the one and only department of a corporation that determines that corporation's wealth, it certainly is one of the most important. When we recognize successful corporations, we are recognizing expertise in budgeting, cost and expense minimization, tax minimization, investment acumen…. The CFO is a critical component of the success or failure of the corporation and how well he/she does their job can be the difference between profit or loss, growth or bankruptcy.

The point is someone needs to be your family's Chief Financial Officer. If your family does not have a CFO then who is looking after the budgeting, cost and expense and tax minimization? Who is going to be on the look-out for whether your little 'corporation' is on track for profit or loss, for growth or bankruptcy?

Educate yourself on as many financial aspects as you can and take action, because the better off you as an individual Canadian are, the better off we all are.

"Don't tell me what you value; show me your budget, and I'll tell you what you value."

- Joe Biden

The Sequential Approach

So maybe we don't have the benefit of having learned the basic lessons of wealth creation that the wealthy have known for years, we interact on a daily basis with corporations which do not have our best interests at heart, we're increasingly getting taxed up the wazoo, and our pensions are questionable at best. And yet, if we haven't become fully conscious of all these realities by now we certainly have had an inkling for a long time that no one is out there taking care of us; no one out there is genuinely concerned about *our* financial well-being. There are no huge secrets here. But we haven't actually done a whole lot to change anything because we have bigger fish to fry a lot closer to home.

We Canadians generally have two pretty pressing financial goals. Firstly, we have this big, ugly mortgage that takes a huge cut off our paycheque every two weeks. And it's relentless. We naturally want this big debt gone as fast as possible.

The second pressing financial issue we have is that we know we need to save for our retirement. We don't want to work forever. We want to be able to actually stop working at some point (or at least drastically slow down) and enjoy our golden years; travel a bit more or play with the grandkids.

And, as mentioned earlier, it is conventional practice in Canada to attack these two goals sequentially. We decide to first concentrate on paying off our mortgage and then once that's gone, that freed-up monthly mortgage payment can go toward saving for our retirement.

Mortgage First, Then Retirement Savings?

Firstly, what's the problem with that? Well, I guess there isn't a huge problem – at least you have recognized that such a large and costly liability is likely best gotten rid of. And if you were able to only do one or the other, depending on current rates, it may be best to first attack the mortgage debt rather than save for retirement. But one of the reasons you may be considered right for deciding to attack the mortgage first is a reason that you probably haven't even considered – that mortgage debt is *not* tax-deductible. A goodly portion of that big monthly mortgage payment goes right to the bank in the form of interest – the price you pay for the privilege of borrowing their money – and you see nothing in return, so the sooner it's gone, the better off we are, right?

Retirement Savings First, Then Mortgage?

But hold on – some of you out there are going to say that it's best to pay the mortgage off over the course of time by making only the minimum required payments and instead start saving for retirement whenever you can rather than applying any extra dollars as mortgage prepayments. After all, if I have a 4% mortgage but I can make 6%, 8%, 10% return by investing, I'm making the positive spread on the dollars I invest rather than directing those extra dollars toward the mortgage. And you might be right. If I take an extra dollar and pay down 4% money, I am necessarily *not* getting that dollar invested at 7% and I am losing the spread.

But here's the fun part about the whole debate around which goal is better to attack first, and it's like watching two guys in the boxing ring: While blue corner is pounding on red corner that concentrating on paying down the mortgage is the best move, and red corner is trying to beat blue corner into agreeing that saving for retirement is the way to go, it is, to a large degree, moot in the first place.

The Debate Can Stop Now

Why is it moot? Well, let's start with the fact that for many Canadians, they only have a set amount of dollars each month, and if half or close to half of their money is going to taxes and another 35-40% on food, shelter and clothing and then the rest is spent on summer camp for Kenny and hockey gear for Heather, where is there meaningful money to invest in the first place? It's just not there, so the default is to concentrate on the mortgage, which by contract must be serviced, rather than invest, which is 'optional'.

Another reason the argument is moot is because they're both right. Both goals can be worked at *simultaneously*. You don't have to make the decision about whether to focus on the mortgage or focus on retirement savings. Do both at the same time.

I tell you it is quite interesting to be observing this debate whenever it opens up in the personal finance world and we have one side showing math that proves one argument and the other side with their own math. We can tackle these issues in tandem; we aren't restricted to tackling these problems in sequential fashion. So take the gloves off and hit the showers and everyone go get a Red Truck IPA and turn the game on.

The debate can stop now.

But before I explain how we can tackle these goals at the same time, let's see where the sequential approach gets us – the conventional practice of first paying out the mortgage and only then starting to save for retirement.

The Canadian Dream

Let's look at Gary and Susan and their 'Canadian Dream'. They bought their first house a while back at 25 years old with a $200,000 mortgage that they managed to pay down a little, raised two kids and got a dog. Susan got promoted and Gary also started to make a little more money as his career progressed. Gary and Susan are both currently 40 years old and lead a decent life now in a comfortable house they just bought with a $300,000 mortgage at 5% amortized over 25 years.

Gary and Susan quite frequently have conversations about how life seems to just get more expensive and the fact that, while they are making more money than they were in the past, the cost of living has kept pace and they still can't seem to get ahead. They manage to pay their bills, keep their daughter, Heather, in decent goalie pads and send Kenny to camp every year, but there's always too much month at the end of their money and they simply don't have any cash to invest for their retirement. They take some comfort, however, in the fact that they are able to pay all their bills, have decent credit scores, there's food on the table, the mortgage payments are up to date and every once in a while they are able to treat themselves to a nice steak dinner or a week in the sun with the kidlets. All things considered, they think they're doing okay. They actually feel, like many other Canadians in the same circumstance, that they will be able to attain the Canadian Dream. And it looks like this:

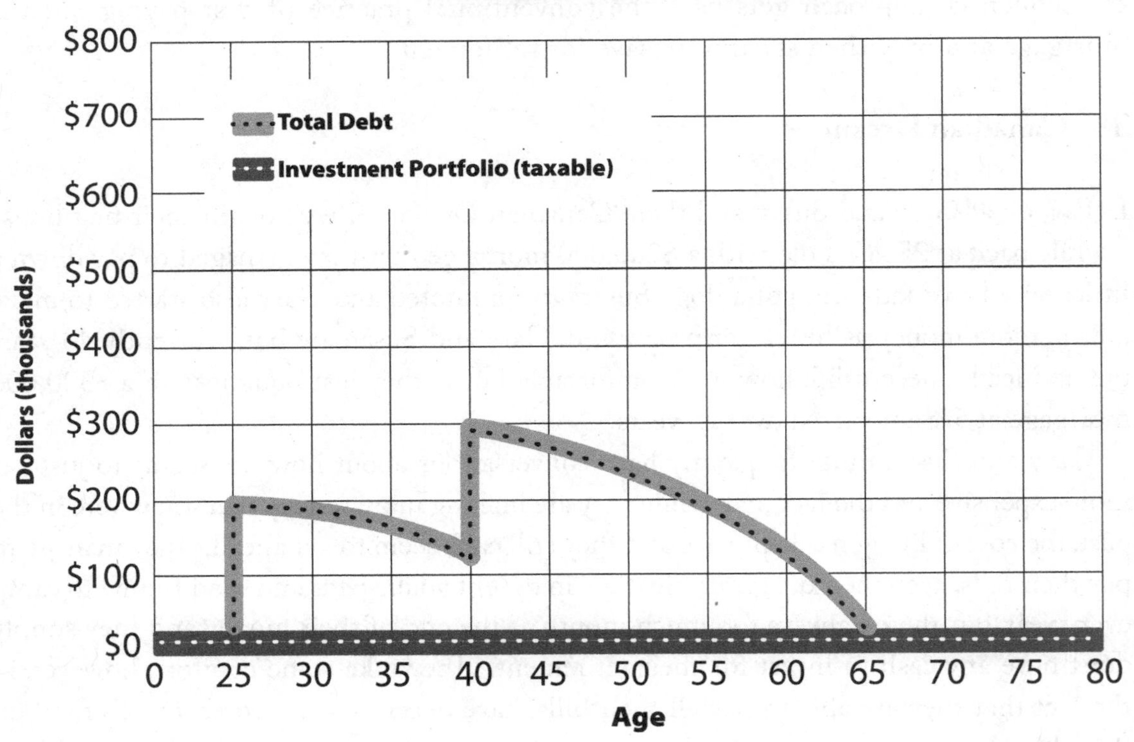

Fig 2.4

Sure, they wish they were a bit better off, who doesn't, but they feel they are doing quite well and are on track. Their plan was, and always has been, to retire on the day they turn age 65 and also have their mortgage fully paid off on the same day, and they are on their way to accomplishing that as far as they can tell. After all, once their mortgage is paid off they won't have that payment burden any more.

Canadian Dream Accomplished!

So let's fast-forward 25 years. Gary and Susan did it! They executed their plan and managed to be both mortgage-free and retired when they hit 65 years old. Gary and Susan have a well-deserved dual-purpose party. They invite all their friends and family and Gary shows off the gold watch his firm gave him at his retirement party that afternoon in the cafeteria and Susan holds up the mortgage papers and ceremoniously throws them into the fireplace. The guests send up a cheer as the mortgage papers go up in smoke and his buddies clap Gary on the back. Susan drains a shot of Patrón and lays a big kiss on Gary's best friend. The Canadian Dream accomplished! Retirement and no more mortgage payments at age 65, exactly as planned.

Well, the next morning Gary and Susan wake up feeling like six pounds of garbage stuffed into a four-pound bag (it was a helluva party!) and after giving the house a quick once-over and popping a Tylenol, they sit at the kitchen table with a cup of coffee to do the math. The realization hits them like a slap in the earhole – there's not going to be enough cash flow in their newfound retirement. Uh oh.

The Canadian Nightmare

Their Canadian Dream has turned into the Canadian Nightmare. And it looks like this:

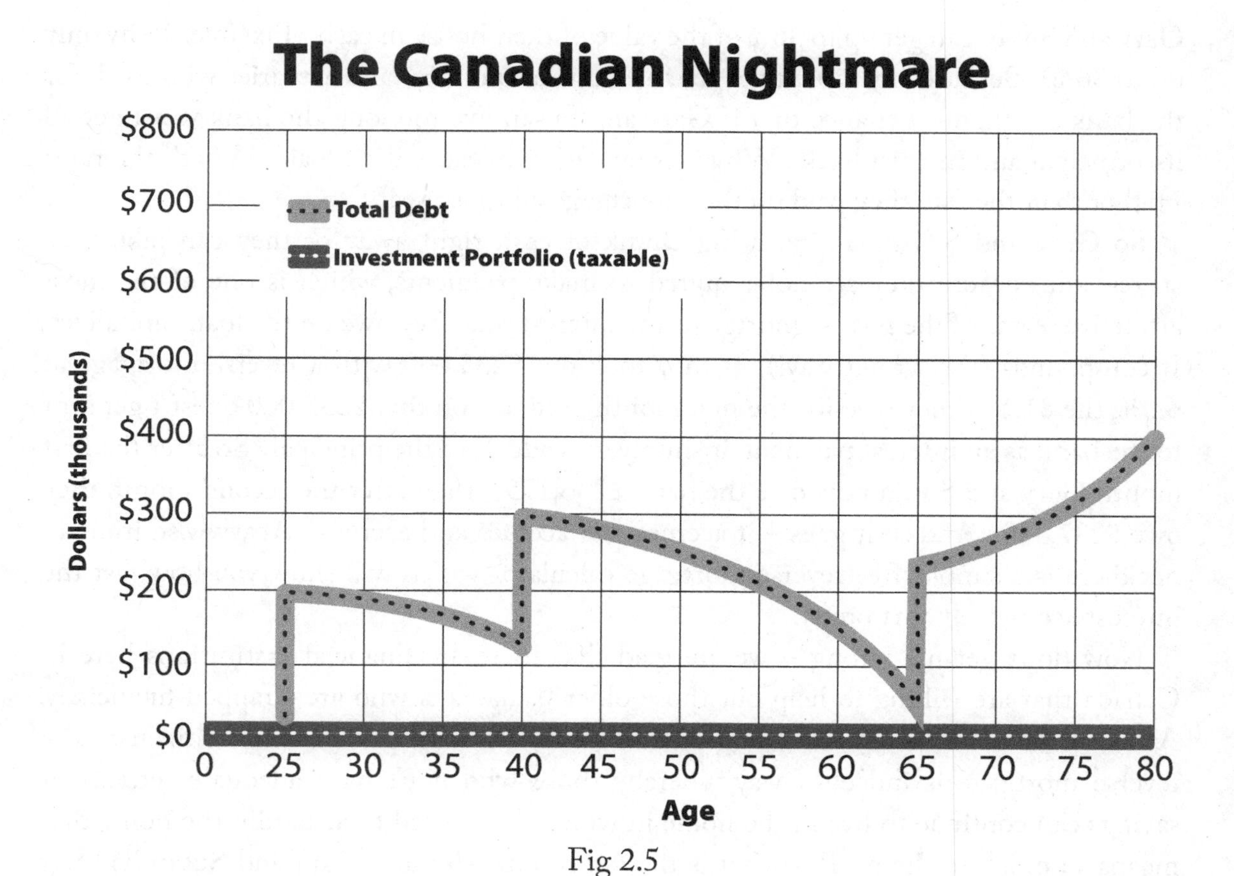

Fig 2.5

Many years ago, Gary and Susan arranged their financial affairs just like everyone around them did because that's how they were taught by everyone who 'knew' how they should do it. They focused on paying out their mortgage and banked on not having that mortgage payment anymore which would free up the cash flow for them to enjoy a decent retirement, but that's not going to work. The relentlessly increasing cost of living has conspired against them, not to mention the fact that they are no longer receiving paycheques. However, they have heard about the reverse mortgage program so they give them a call. They allow Gary and Susan to sign up but the price is steep.

"A nickel ain't worth a dime anymore."
- Yogi Berra

The Reverse Mortgage

Gary and Susan can get up to 36% of the value of their house in cash. Tax-free. Why only up to 36%? Because any more than that and the accountants and actuaries who work for the bank say there's a chance that if Gary and Susan live too long the bank won't get all its principal and interest back. Why is it tax-free? Because it's a loan. What's the rate? Higher than the rate they paid on their mortgage all those years.

So Gary and Susan can get a big chunk of cash right away or they can take it in stages, but because they are not required to make payments, which is one of the most attractive terms of the reverse mortgage, the interest that they owe on the loan capitalizes. It compounds (the wrong way!) If they took out $235,000 with a reverse mortgage at 6.0%, the $1,175 they owe for the first month's interest on that $235,000 doesn't get sent to the bank as an interest payment, it simply gets added to the principal. So after the first month Gary and Susan now owe the bank $236,175. Then after the second month they owe $237,350. And so it goes – it accrues and accrues and accrues. At www.smithman.net there is a simple, free reverse mortgage calculator which will show you how fast the interest accrues. It ain't pretty.

Now don't get me wrong – we are glad that there are financial institutions here in Canada that are willing to help out those older Canadians who are strapped financially. After all, who else would be willing to lend money to unemployed senior citizens? The reverse mortgage is indeed a way whereby those who don't have adequate retirement savings can continue to live in the home in which they raised their family, the home that means so much to them. But what is the net result? Because Gary and Susan had not saved up funds to support their retirement, they didn't have any savings to leave Kenny and Heather. And not only that, once Gary and Susan leave this world their kids won't get the house either – the bank will. Maybe not all of it, but a good deal of it. Or...maybe all of it...

Bank-Owned Day One and Bank-Owned at the Very End

In the end, Gary and Susan were under the thumb of the bank for almost their whole lives. They worked for the bank starting at age 25 when they bought their first house, they were clear of the bank for one day when they hit 65 years old retiring mortgage-free, and then the next day they effectively started selling the house back to the bank via the reverse mortgage because they were short on savings and cash flow. Their home equity ended up financing their retirement and this is not inherently 'wrong', but there is more than one way to make your home equity work for you. You can either use the equity in your home *now* with *The Smith Manoeuvre* and let the magic of compound growth work *for* your retirement plan, or you can forego compound growth and store the equity in your home to sell your house back to the bank later *in* your retirement.

Think of it this way – all of your adult life you will be working for money in order to be able to *increase* the amount of money that the bank will lend to you via a reverse mortgage. This is worth repeating: *The more of your hard-earned, after-tax dollars that you apply against your mortgage throughout the years, the more the bank will be able to lend you at a rate very likely higher than your original mortgage.*

The most recent statistics are out and the uptake for reverse mortgages in Canada is increasing around 30% per year. This is a direct testament to the inability of more and more Canadians to adequately prepare for their retirement. If they were adequately prepared would they be selling their house back to the bank? No, they would not.

Make your mortgage and home equity work for you *now* so that it can create wealth for you. Don't wait for 15, 20, 25 years while that home equity moulders at 0% growth only to use it to take out a loan in retirement whereby the bank starts to own more and more of your home each and every month. Remember this when someone tells you that they think it's best that you be mortgage-free and have lots of equity in your house that can help you in retirement.

Help you? Or the bank?

The Value of Professional Advice

So we have had quite a bit of discussion to this point about what others know that we don't and the multitude of forces working against our financial success. But we can turn this around, folks.

If you have not already, book some time with a financial advisor and chances are he or she will be able to show you how to create at least a little bit more wealth for you than you could generate by yourself. After all, this is what they do for a living and why they have the expensive degrees on the wall and a bunch of letters beside their name on their business card.

It really does not take much to design a plan that, if you stick with it, will at least get you on the road to improved net worth that otherwise you wouldn't have found by yourself. Regardless how much you are putting away at this point in time, chances are high that it could be a little more if you had a bit of help from a pro.

In fact, you already have the opportunity to increase your wealth even though you may not have realized it. The very fact that you are reading this book tells me that you either have a house and a mortgage now or likely will at some point in the near future. And while owning a house and taking on the mortgage and the monthly payment that comes with it may seem like you are a little worse off on a cash flow basis than before you had a house and mortgage payment, you can turn that mortgage payment into wealth.

Your Mortgage Is Offering to Help - Don't Ignore It!

Say I have a $2,600 monthly mortgage payment. And let's say $1,600 of that goes to the bank in interest expense – the price I pay for the privilege of borrowing that money. When that $1,600 goes to the bank it is gone. I do not see any of that money ever again; I don't get to enjoy anything further from the fact that I sent the bank that $1,600. I do see benefit in the fact that I now own $1,000 more of my house than I did the month previous, but that $1,600 that went to the mortgage lender is gone. And guess what – I get to send them more money next month. And the next...

But let's talk about the $1,000 that reduces the amount I owe to the bank. I have just created $1,000 in additional equity in the house for myself. Excellent – feels good to see that big, ugly loan balance reduce each month; granted, at a very slow pace. But reduce, it does.

So, if I just paid down my mortgage by $1,000 and created $1,000 of additional equity in that house, what is it doing for me? How is that $1,000 increasing my net worth not just this month, but next month and the month after and for the many, many months going forward that I am going to be living in my house? Nothing. That $1,000 of home equity is not in any sort of investment vehicle. Heck, it's not even in a bank account earning one percent. And if that $1,000 from my very first mortgage payment is earning 0% the first month, it is also earning 0% the second month and the next month and every month thereafter. For as long as I own my house, whether I am still making mortgage payments or not, that $1,000 will earn me precisely 0%. I am not even getting a bank account savings rate, and I am certainly not even keeping up to inflation.

And not only that, the original $1,000 that reduced the mortgage balance earns 0% for as long as I own the house, but the second $1,000 or so that reduces the mortgage balance *also* earns 0% for as long as I own the house and the third $1,000 and so on. Pretty soon I have tens of thousands, then hundreds of thousands of dollars that are mine but have never earned me a single penny.

But I have the ability to generate investment-grade returns on the dollars by which my mortgage payment reduces the balance, each and every month, without requiring any more cash from my income.

Turn Your Mortgage into Money

At this point, some people might be arguing that the dollars by which I reduce my mortgage balance, and therefore increase the amount of the house I actually own rather than the bank, will in fact be doing some work because I can reasonably expect the house to increase in value over time. And I can see where this thought process would come from, but think about it this way – let's say I buy a $500,000 house with a $400,000 mortgage and after 25 years the house is worth $800,000 and I now owe nothing against it. Well ignoring the enormous cost of the mortgage (not only interest payments but the fact that I had to use after-tax dollars to make those payments) I feel I have done pretty well. If I sold the house I would get $800,000 for something I paid $500,000 for. Not bad.

But what if I were able to pull the equity from the house as fast as I was creating it with my mortgage payments and get it invested? If those investments were valued at $850,000 after the 25 years I've owned my house and I still owed the bank $400,000, then if I sold my investments to pay back the investment loan secured by my house, I would have, pre-tax, $450,000 in cash and a clear title house worth $800,000. So, after 25 years, instead of having a net worth of $800,000 to enjoy, I would have $1,250,000 to enjoy. And that is much more enjoyier, I think you'll agree.

CHAPTER 3

THE SMITH MANOEUVRE EXPLAINED

Okay, time to get down to the nitty gritty on process and functionality. How does *The Smith Manoeuvre* actually work? What is the process? In a nutshell, whatever equity you generate in your house via the reduction of the mortgage balance due to the regular mortgage payment, you are going to reborrow to invest each month into a non-registered investment account.

This reborrowing to invest leads to tax deductions because you are borrowing with the reasonable expectation of earning income. These tax deductions are calculated at tax time and the result is that over the course of the past 12 months you have paid too much tax – when the government was taking their share off your paycheque every two weeks they were doing so based on your estimated income exclusive of any tax deductions. So, because you have these valuable tax deductions the Canada Revenue Agency (CRA) has to send you money back at tax time. There's your refund.

And when the resulting tax refunds arrive each year you are going to prepay the mortgage by that amount and then reborrow it as well in order to invest. That's it. But first you need to restructure so that you will be able to access that monthly increase in equity. You need a readvanceable mortgage.

The Readvanceable Mortgage

Let's say I am buying a $500,000 house. After consulting a *Smith Manoeuvre Certified Professional* mortgage broker, we put in an application for a readvanceable mortgage at 80% loan-to-value. I am approved and with a $100,000 down payment and a $400,000 mortgage that house becomes mine('ish). That first night I am unable to get to sleep due to a combination of elation and sheer panic, but that's neither here nor there. But what is a readvanceable mortgage and why do I need one? Let's start with what people typically think of when they think 'mortgage'. A typical mortgage looks like figure 3.1:

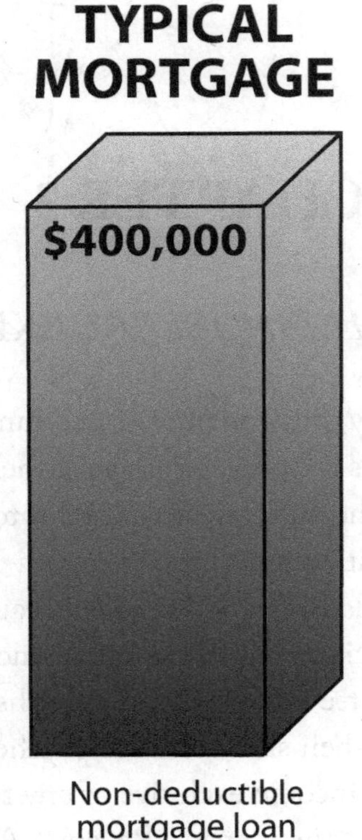

Fig. 3.1

A typical mortgage is simply one big lump sum of money that is borrowed from the bank that you are expected to pay back over a set period of time by making principal-plus-interest payments at an interest rate that is either fixed for a term or variable. We make regular – usually monthly – payments on this loan and whatever does not go to the bank in interest payments, goes to reduce the amount we owe. The balance comes down slowly over time, maybe 25 or 30 years depending on the original amortization schedule, and eventually it is all paid back to the bank and we own our house outright. Happy days (until we realize we need to sign up for that reverse mortgage).

Readvanceable = Opportunity

But a readvanceable mortgage is different. Not all readvanceable mortgages function or look identical, but they generally have the common characteristic of having at least one other facility attached to that amortizing loan portion of a typical mortgage described above. So, in addition to the principal-plus-interest amortizing loan component (the 'mortgage'), we will see at least one secured line of credit but sometimes more depending on the lender, and as the house is collateral, you enjoy the best rates around. The following explanation is quite basic considering different total loan percentages vary depending on the type of readvanceable mortgage component, but your *Smith Manoeuvre Certified Professional* mortgage broker will be able to break it down depending on which lender you are looking at (this is in relation to the 65% LTV rule I discuss later on).

A readvanceable mortgage is basically an agreement by the bank to always allow you to have owing to the bank the amount of the original total loan, should you wish. If I borrow $400,000 day one to buy my house, the bank is okay with me always owing them $400,000.

So a readvanceable mortgage effectively looks like figure 3.2:

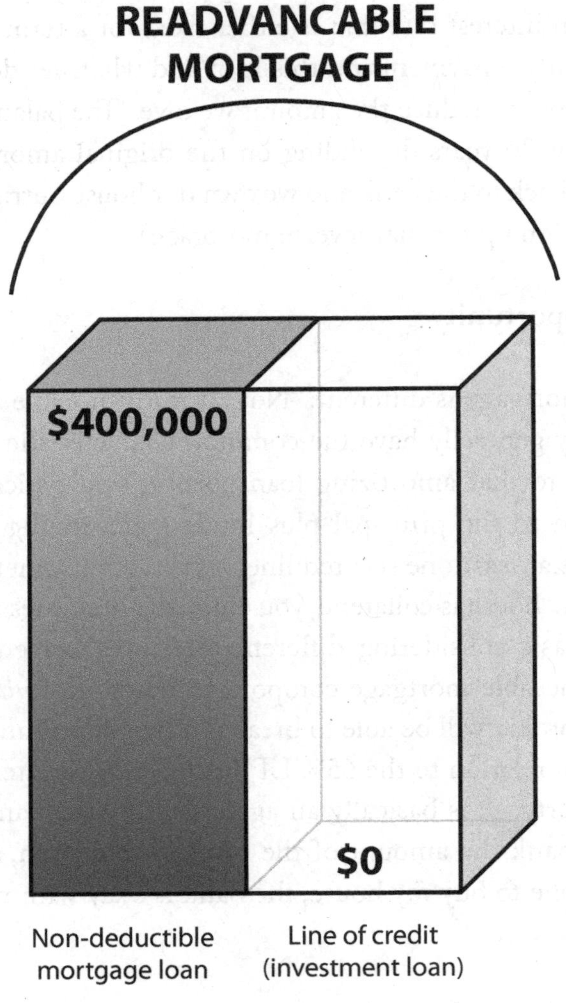

Fig. 3.2

In figure 3.2 I have a $400,000 amortizing mortgage loan and a line of credit with a $0 limit. Why $0? Because my total loan is $400,000 and therefore there is no available credit on the line. I have borrowed to my maximum on the loan portion because I needed all of it plus my $100,000 down payment to purchase the $500,000 house.

The defining characteristic of a readvanceable is that whenever the principal balance on the amortizing loan portion – that initial $400,000 of borrowing that allowed me to buy my house – is reduced by the principal component of my mortgage payment, the line of credit limit will increase dollar for dollar therefore allowing me to reborrow whatever new equity my payment on the loan portion created.

The Bank's Rationale

Why is the bank willing to offer me a readvanceable mortgage which means that they may be owed the full amount of original borrowing forever?

- They ran the math the day they took my mortgage application and figured that considering my credit score, occupation, winsome smile, net worth, income, etc., I could handle the payment on a $400,000 loan balance.

- If they were willing to lend me $400,000 at qualification last month, what has changed that they would not be willing to lend me $400,000 the next month? Or the next? And so on? Nothing. Nothing has changed.

- Their asset – the total loan – likely never diminishes, which they like.

- They have the house as security for the loan, which is very safe. Further, I had to put in at least 20% of my own cash as a down payment, so there is already lots of equity in the house to account for any short-term negative fluctuations in the house value.

Trust me – the bank is very comfortable with the arrangement. Don't worry about the bank, dear Reader.

So now I have a new $400,000 readvanceable mortgage and I make my first mortgage payment of $2,100. Out of that $2,100 payment, let's say $1,320 goes to line the pockets of the bankers in the form of interest – non-deductible for me. That leaves $780 to reduce the principal. So, after that $780 reduction registers I now have a loan portion balance of $399,220. That being the case, because I have a readvanceable mortgage and the lender has agreed to always allow me to owe them a total of $400,000, the line of credit limit increases from $0 to $780. I can then reborrow that $780 into my bank account and do whatever I wish with it. What we actually *do* with that reborrowed money is fundamental to either wealth creation or wealth erosion, but suffice it to say at this point, we are not going to make a Lexus payment with it. After I reborrow that $780, the image of the readvanceable mortgage looks like figure 3.3:

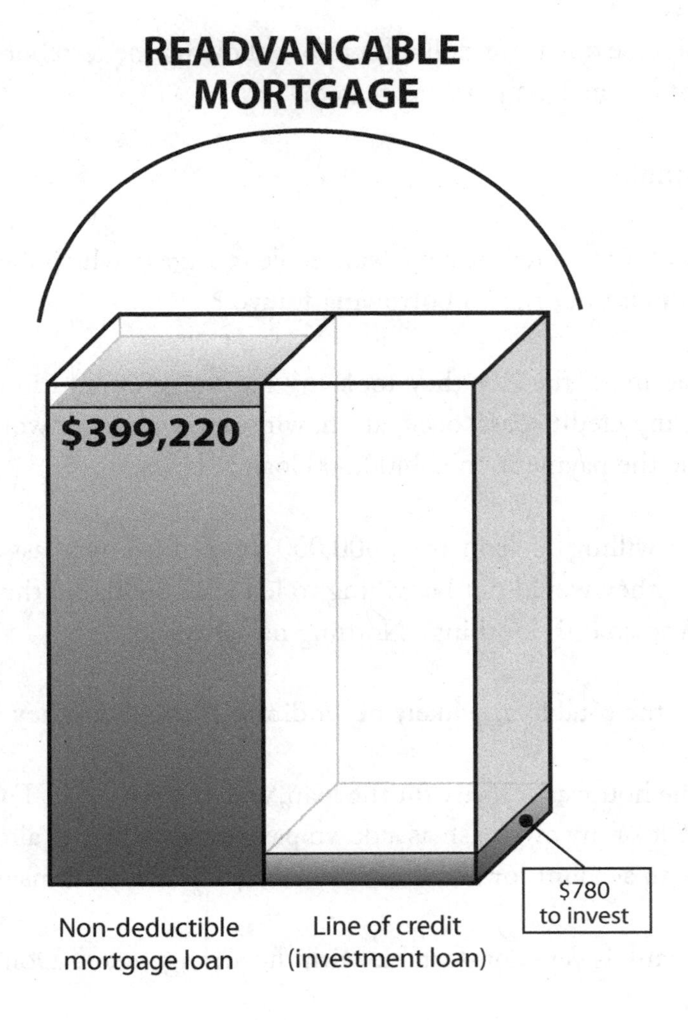

Fig. 3.3

When we add the two sides we still get a total balance of $400,000 just like the day I got the mortgage a month ago. The next month I am again able to reborrow whatever principal is reduced by the principal portion of the mortgage payment and so on. Eventually, if I stick at it, the mortgage will look like figure 3.4:

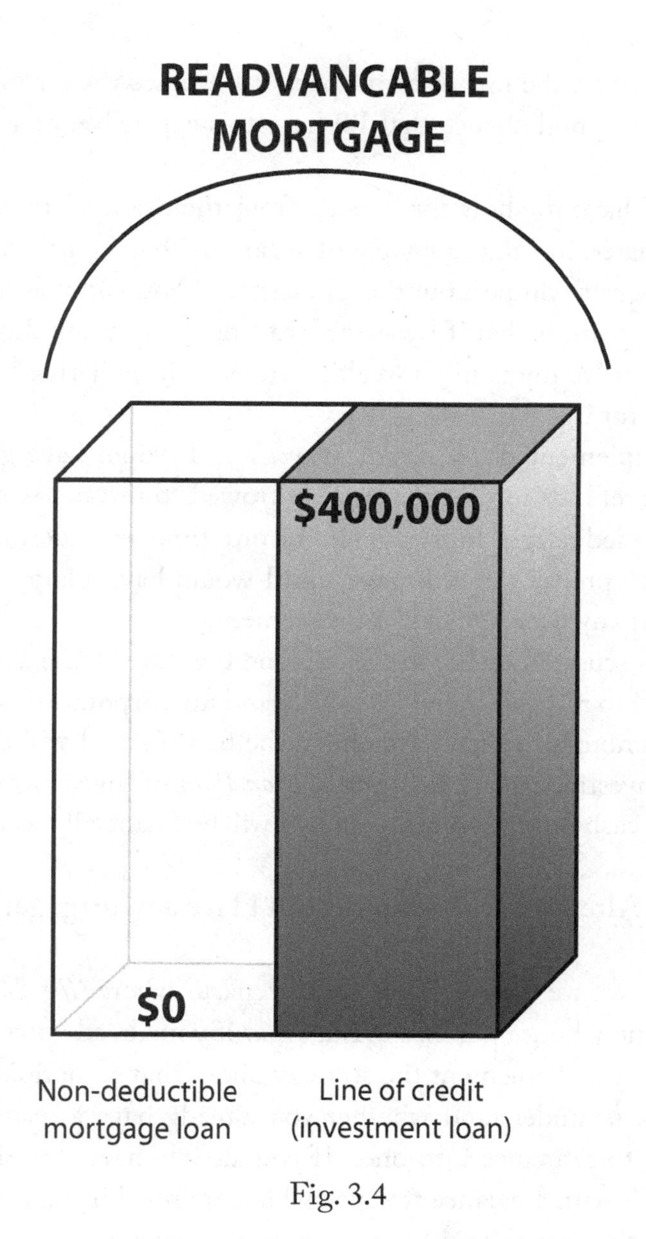

Fig. 3.4

Be Careful How You Use the Readvanceable Mortgage

So what have I accomplished with the above? Well, if I was not implementing *The Smith Manoeuvre* and actually *did* use the newly available credit each month to make a Lexus payment, go on some vacations and fancy dinners throughout the years, then I have managed to replace $400,000 of *non-deductible* debt on the loan portion with $400,000 of *non-deductible* debt on the line of credit portion. And as the payments on the line are interest-only, there's a good chance that I'll have this expensive, non-deductible debt for life.

And what will I have to show for it aside from the draining monthly payments? A car that has depreciated in value, a couple of vacations that I enjoyed but now only have photographs of, expensive dinners out that got eaten.... You know the old saying, "Leasing the lifestyle..." The point is that if I was reborrowing to consume this whole time, I have done nothing to improve my family's wealth – in fact I have harmed it – and I have next to nothing to show for it.

However, if I implemented *The Smith Manoeuvre* I would have giant tax deductions leading to giant tax refunds for life because I borrowed to *invest*, I would have eliminated the expensive non-deductible mortgage in record time considering these annual tax refunds were used to prepay the mortgage, and I would have a large pool of investments which I can enjoy at any time, typically in retirement.

Remember our discussion earlier in the book on the state of Canadian pensions? Well, I no longer will have to rely solely on CPP, OAS, and my corporate or government pension plan, if I am lucky enough to even have one in the first place. I will have a large nest egg of free-and-clear investments – a *Personal Pension Plan* of my very own – with which to generate additional cash flow in my retirement. I will be financially secure and comfortable.

But What If You Already Own a House and Have a Mortgage?

In the example above, we were looking at a scenario where *The Smith Manoeuvre* was implemented on a new house purchase. But what if you already own a home and have a mortgage? How do you implement the strategy under that scenario?

Well, first check to understand whether you already have a readvanceable mortgage or if you will need to refinance into one. If you already have a readvanceable, you may need to restructure it with a balance transfer, which entails shifting over any existing non-deductible debt on the line of credit portion you may have previously borrowed for non-deductible consumption to add to the non-deductible principal-plus-interest amortizing loan portion remaining on your mortgage. This can be done for zero cost to you and a *Smith Manoeuvre Certified Professional* will know what to do. We also go through this in more detail in *The Smith Manoeuvre Homeowner Course*. By executing this balance transfer you can start with a zero-balance line of credit and not have to worry about mixing the two types of debt – non-deductible and deductible. That would be a very bad idea from the perspective of being able to track valuable deductible interest going forward. Do not mix debt!

If you don't already have a readvanceable mortgage then you need to refinance into one. Speak with a *Smith Manoeuvre Certified Professional* mortgage broker. You can expect the typical financing costs but they can mostly or fully be rolled into the new mortgage so that you may need not pay anything out of pocket at refinance. Your broker will walk you through the whole process.

Monthly Process

Alright, so at this point we know that we need a readvanceable mortgage and that we are going to reborrow any monthly reduction in the non-deductible amortizing loan portion of the mortgage in order to invest so that we are starting to save for our future *now*. This starts to generate valuable tax deductions *now* and, at a minimum, we will prepay the mortgage with these annual tax refunds *each year* to quickly eliminate this non-deductible mortgage.

So how does this all actually happen? We first need to make sure that we have our bank accounts structured appropriately and this will most likely occur with the help of your accredited *Smith Manoeuvre Certified Professional* mortgage broker and *Smith Manoeuvre Certified Professional* real estate lawyer or notary on the day your mortgage goes through. But what you want is this: your existing bank account – we call this your *'Personal Chequing Account'* – is connected to the amortizing loan portion of the mortgage which is the non-deductible mortgage loan that you will be paying down over time. This is the $400,000 in our example above that you borrowed day one in order to buy the house.

And this *Personal Chequing Account* is the chequing account you've always had – your employment income goes into this account, you pay for your groceries and gas from this account, you have been making your old mortgage payments from this account, etc. Nothing new here. You will be required to identify which account you want the mortgage lender to come into every month/two weeks/week in order to take the mortgage payment and this will be that account. Easy peasy.

However, you will also be asked to which account you want the attached secured readvanceable line of credit (or other readvancing facility of the mortgage) linked. If you are not asked this question, it is likely that everyone is assuming you want the existent *Personal Chequing Account* also linked to the line of credit – the same account from which the regular mortgage payments will be automatically taken. So make sure that you specify you want a different account linked to the line of credit. This is a new account that you will want to open at your bank.

Bank Account Segregation

This is critical: you will open this new chequing account – *The Smith Manoeuvre Chequing Account* – specifically for the purposes of implementing *The Smith Manoeuvre* and you will use this new account for absolutely nothing else. Make a promise to yourself to follow this rule. *Do not use this new account for anything other than The Smith Manoeuvre process.* It is important because any funds that will be going *into* that account will be coming from the line of credit and therefore will be borrowed funds. Any funds going *out* of that account will be going towards deductible uses of borrowed funds only.

In order to stay onside with the CRA, you will need to be able to show very clearly, if ever asked, the direct and unpolluted line of travel and use of borrowed money. You will want to be able to show a direct path of money borrowed from the line of credit going into the new *Smith Manoeuvre Chequing Account* and then this money going out of this account for only investment or payment of deductible investment loan interest.

Bearing in mind that some readvanceable mortgages have varying features/functionality, figure 3.5 is a graphic representation of what things should look like if set up correctly:

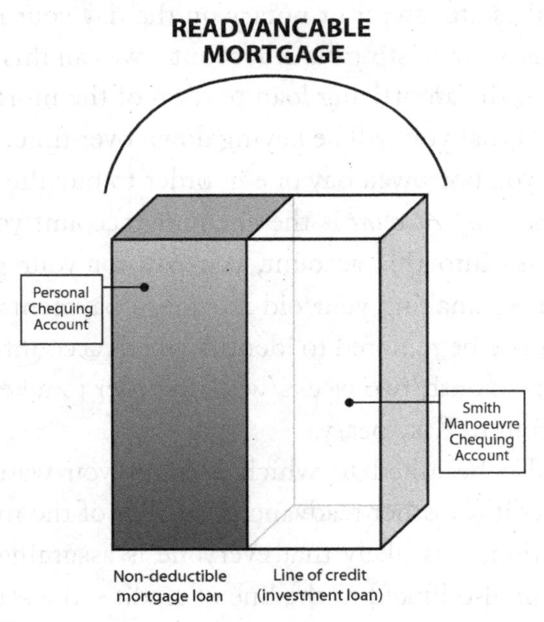

Fig. 3.5

You're Ready to Go!

Once the bank accounts are linked correctly to the various components of the readvanceable mortgage, you are ready to get going. Apart from the implementation of the various accelerators to be discussed shortly, the base-case scenario is that your regular mortgage payment will continue, of course, but you will withdraw any newly available credit after it is made available considering the principal reduction of the mortgage due to the mortgage payment.

On a monthly basis, the payment to cover any interest expense on the deductible line of credit will automatically be taken by your mortgage lender (they'll make sure of that!), but what about the monthly investment contribution? You will have a discussion with your accredited *Smith Manoeuvre Certified Professional* investment advisor about which types of investments are appropriate for you, and the final decision is entirely yours, but whatever decision you come to, you will want to set it up so that the monthly investment from the dedicated *Smith Manoeuvre Chequing Account* occurs automatically, if at all possible. Whether it's $500, $1,000, $2,000 or more, you want to make sure that this monthly investment contribution occurs automatically without constant monthly instruction from you.

If instructing this monthly investment instalment requires action from you on an ongoing basis, there is a danger that you miss it here or there, or for a few months. This is expensive and can cause some issues with your deduction claim. You want to make this whole program runs as automatically as possible and with as little ongoing action from you. Make it easy on yourself – automate the monthly investment.

And considering that you are generating more and more tax deductions each month because you are borrowing to invest, you can expect the CRA to be very generous at tax time. *The Smithman Calculator* will calculate (as calculators tend to do) the tax effect of these deductions for you. So when you receive your tax refund each year, you will apply it against the principal balance of the mortgage and then get this amount reborrowed and invested. Be disciplined about this – the tax refunds you are receiving are coming to you only because of *The Smith Manoeuvre*.

Historically you may have always gotten back a refund, but you will see an increase in the amount once you start converting your mortgage, all else being equal. If you hadn't engaged in the strategy you would not be receiving these refunds anyway, so use them, or at least the incremental amount, to convert your mortgage as fast as possible.

If Any Mortgage Lenders Are Reading This Right Now, Feel Free to Give Me a Call…

You may have already seen the quote from Larry Bell, former VanCity CEO – "Why isn't every Canadian doing this?" I'll mention at this point for clarity that VanCity does not offer a true readvanceable mortgage, in fact, they never really did. The system that Fraser and the kind folk at VanCity put into place way back when was restricted by the technology of the day, cumbersome and very administratively involved and tedious. Effective, but tedious. Soon after VanCity started winning new clients by offering to collaborate with Fraser, the big banks started to develop readvanceable mortgages – types of mortgages which would auto-readvance – and they have been improving them ever since.

While VanCity does not currently have a product that works smoothly for *The Smith Manoeuvre*, a number of mortgage lenders do. In *The Smith Manoeuvre Homeowner Course* we look at readvanceable mortgages from a number of different lenders operating in the mortgage broker channel, the pros and cons of each, and we go into setup and monthly process in more detail.

Some readvanceables are better than others, but none are perfect, so if you are a mortgage lender looking to generate new business from the increasing number of Canadian homeowners implementing *The Smith Manoeuvre*, I'd love to discuss creating the perfect *Smith Manoeuvre Mortgage*.

Summary

So let's summarize this section:

1. Get a readvanceable mortgage.

2. Ensure you have the proper bank accounts linked correctly to the various components of the mortgage.

3. Reborrow any newly available credit after the monthly mortgage payment reduces the non-deductible mortgage balance.

4. Get the funds invested – preferably automatically – each and every month as soon as possible.

5. When you receive your annual tax refund, make an extra prepayment against the mortgage and get that amount reborrowed and invested as well.

Remember, be sure to use accredited *Smith Manoeuvre Certified Professionals (SMCP)* for assistance regarding your *Smith Manoeuvre*; and by 'professionals' I mean real estate agents, mortgage brokers, investment advisors, real estate lawyers/notaries, insurance agents and accountants. If your advisors do not have this *SMCP* designation, then they have not taken the extensive course on the strategy nor have they passed the examination which entitles them to this accreditation.

So, there you go – that's *The Smith Manoeuvre* described in its simplest form, but there is, of course, much more to it. Onward to some scenarios…

CHAPTER 4

LET'S LOOK AT A COUPLE OF RESULTS

So we've gone ahead and secured a readvanceable mortgage, we've set up our bank accounts appropriately, and we're starting the process. Let's look at some examples using *The Smithman Calculator* to see what happens under different scenarios. How will implementing *The Smith Manoeuvre* improve the net worth of typical Canadian homeowners? How could it help you?

Let's Compare

Remember our earlier discussion on the sequential approach? The advice that most of us are given at a young age by someone older and 'wiser' than us to first attack our mortgage debt and once it was gone, start saving for retirement? It is difficult to alter the inertia of many generations passing financial messages down the line over the years. This is especially true when these messages are repeated and reinforced by some financial planners and industry gurus. But let's see what the math says. We need to compare the common sequential approach to debt reduction and investment accrual employed by most mortgage holders in Canada against the potential of *The Smith Manoeuvre.*

Darren and Mark

Let's assume these two gentlemen have just turned 40, and have similar families, training, jobs and aspirations. They each buy nearly identical houses for $500,000, each have mortgages of $400,000 and both are destined to attain the Canadian Dream which is to retire both themselves and their mortgages on their 65th birthday. Their 'Canadian Dream' graph is indicated in figure 4.1.

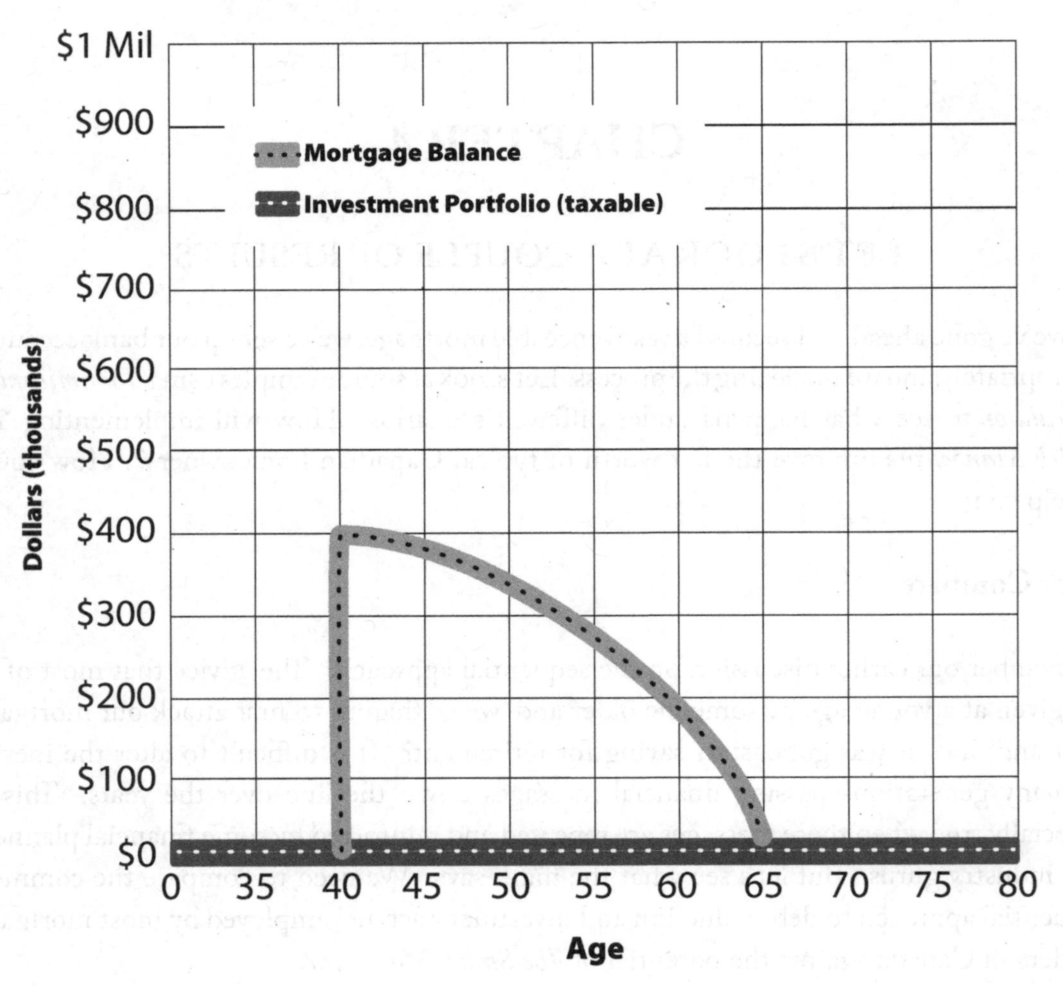

Fig. 4.1

At this point, circumstances are such that they will manage to pay their mortgages off by then but will not have had the means to gather any other assets throughout the years while they were busy paying off their mortgages. But they are currently not too concerned because firstly, retirement seems so far away, and secondly, because they have heard that they can always get this thing called a 'reverse mortgage' at retirement to augment or provide their retirement cash flow.

Darren First

Darren was given a copy of *Master Your Mortgage for Financial Freedom* for his 40th birthday but never picked it up because, well, it's reading, and reading is really hard…, and with his busy life, the only time he had to read, should the inclination strike, just happened to be when his favourite show was on TV. Dancing with the Stars, I think it was. Never missed an episode.

Fast forward 25 years…

Darren originally had a $400,000 mortgage at 4% and managed to pay it off right on schedule the day he retired at age 65. Like most Canadians, Darren didn't have a pension plan tied to his job and adding to this lack of pension plan, his CPP and OAS were not nearly enough to allow him to retire in comfort. Darren had to resort to a reverse mortgage in order to have enough retirement income. The story of his life with mortgage debt is shown in figure 4.2.

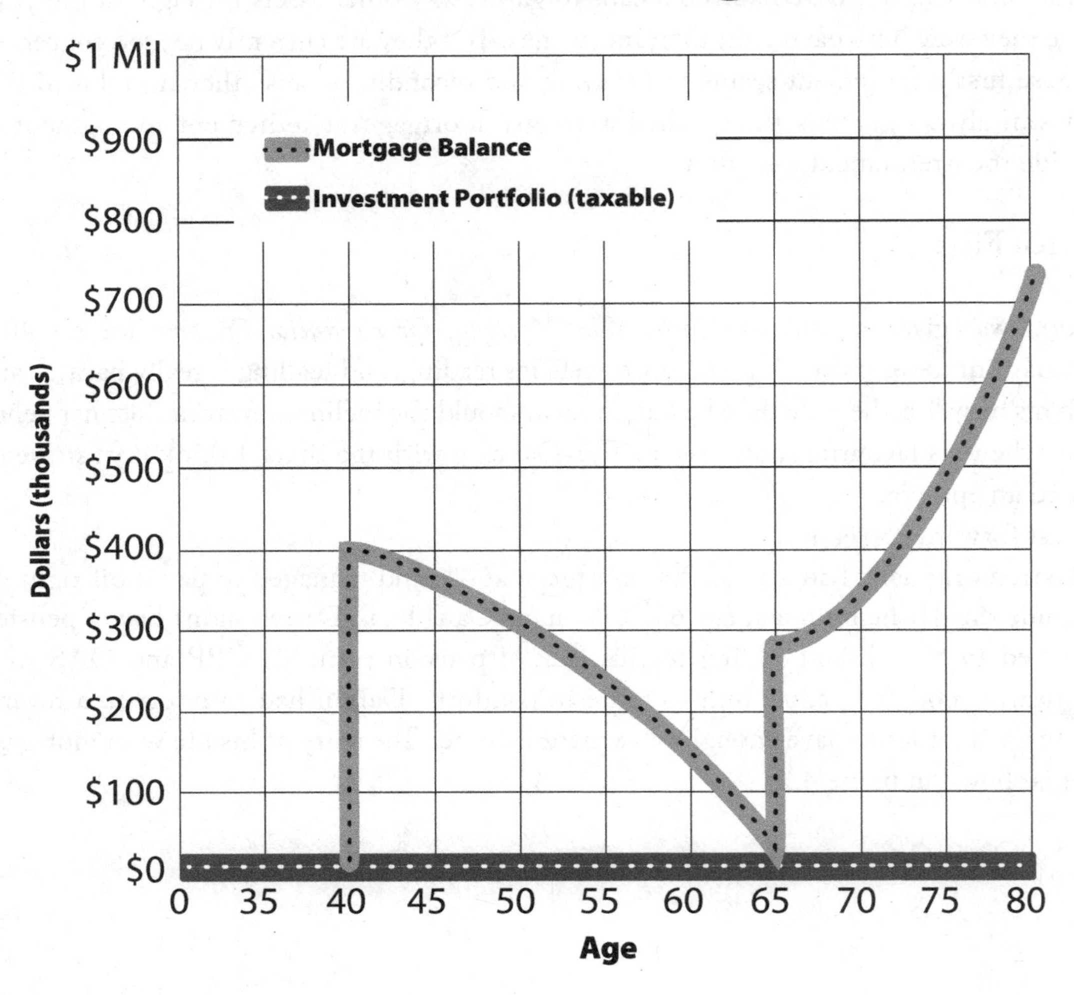

Fig. 4.2

In figure 4.2, we can see Darren got his $400,000 mortgage at age 40 and proceeded to gradually pay it off in full by age 65 (and he had to earn a total of $1,052,040 to pay out that $400,000). However, due to his retirement cash flow deficiency, he had to sign for a reverse mortgage and took the maximum loan of $290,000 in a lump sum. From that point onward, the monthly interest owed on that debt did not get paid by Darren each month, but instead was added to the balance of the original borrowing, and this occurred each month. By the time Darren reached 80 years old, the balance owing the bank was over $722,000.

At Least There Was Someone Darren Could Turn To

Thank goodness the bank was there to give him what he needed. He borrowed $290,000, the maximum he could, and this would hopefully be just enough to keep him somewhat comfortable until he died. The major downside was that his house had little or no equity left in it when he did die. It was sold and most, if not all, of the proceeds went to the bank to pay off the reverse mortgage loan, which was the contract.

In actuality, Darren had been working for the bank from the time he bought his first house with the bank's money at age 40 until he died an old man. The bank owned most of his house at age 40 and again upon his death. In between, he made mortgage payments for 25 years of his life while he worked, with the bank holding his house as security. Then all through his retirement, no longer employed, he lived off the equity in his house that he had worked 25 years to generate.

Again, none of this is improper. Darren was grateful that the bank would lend him most of the money to buy his first house at age 40. He understood that he was really just renting the bank's money and that their job was to earn a return on the investment of their shareholders. Darren was grateful again at age 65 when they loaned him money even though he was unemployed. Yes, they took a premium on the rate, and the costs were stiff, but nobody else was on hand to help out. It's unreasonable to bash the banks for supplying cash when few others are willing or able.

But in the end, from age 40 until his death, his house was free-and-clear of the bank for just one day – his 65th birthday – and then it started going back to the bank.

Mark Bought the Book and *The Smithman Calculator*

And he's glad he did. The most important thing Mark learned from reading the book and speaking with his *Smith Manoeuvre Certified Professional* advisors was that he had the ability to act just as the wealthy do. All he had to do was emulate methods used by successful business and by the wealthy, and he would grow his net worth by thousands and thousands of dollars. All he had to do was realize that the way to much-improved net worth was not by *reducing* his debt, but rather by *converting* it from the bad kind to the good kind by leaving his debt constant at $400,000 during the conversion process. He discovered that the objective is to follow the trail blazed by the wealthy and by businesses who learned a long time ago that you measure wealth by net worth, not by how little debt you have.

The Conversion Process

Figure 4.3 illustrates what Mark did to effect *The Smith Manoeuvre*. The light gray line with the black dots shows the mortgage (bad debt) being amortized. As fast as it drops, the equity is being reborrowed at the same speed in order to invest, represented by the darker line with the white dots (good debt). This means the total of good and bad debt together will add to $400,000 at all times. The debt will remain level. This is represented by the black line with the white dashes.

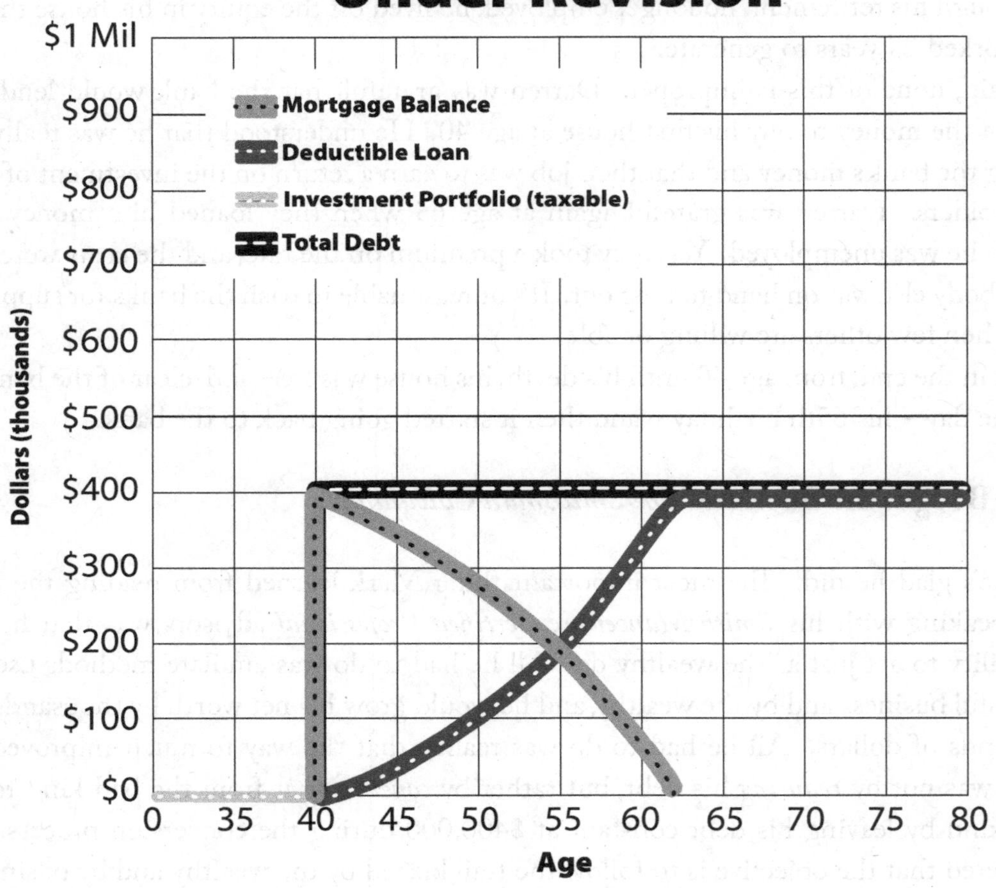

Fig. 4.3

The assets being purchased each month will grow on a compounding basis of 8% per year in this example. The total of the investment portfolio (*Personal Pension Plan*) at Mark's age 65 will have reached $840,394 represented in figure 4.4 by the light gray line with the white dots.

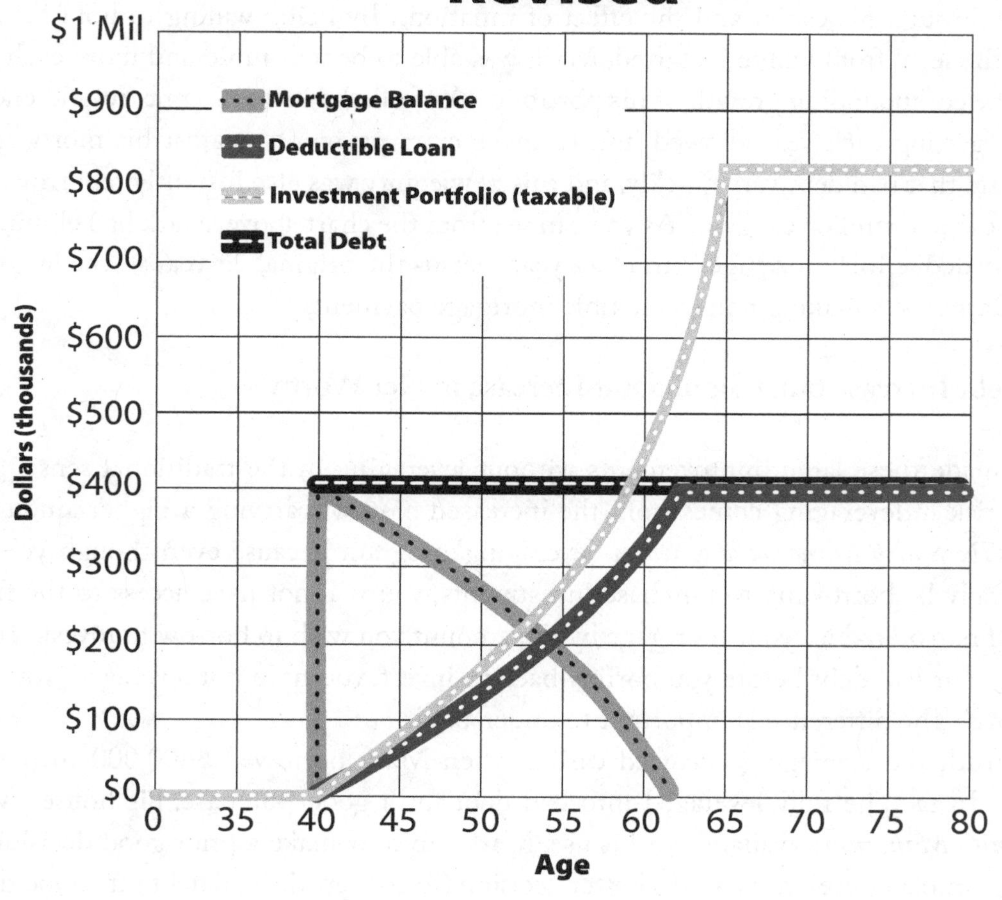

Fig. 4.4

The portfolio total is shown to stay flat at $840,394 from age 65 onward because the assumption is that Mark will convert the portfolio to income production, perhaps dividends, at age 65 when he retires, and he will also continue to enjoy the tax benefits of the deductions.

All Mark had to do to pick up these advantages was to come to understand that he was far further ahead to drop his plan of trying to pay off his mortgage. Instead, as fast as he reduced his mortgage each month, all he had to do was borrow back the same amount to buy more investments for his portfolio. His debt would not increase – it would remain constant.

Mark reckoned that if he could handle his $400,000 mortgage at age 40, it would become ever easier to handle as the years progressed considering increasing income as he moved through his career and the effect of inflation. By being willing to hold his debt flat at the level from where it started, Mark was able to benefit more and more each year from the compounding growth of his portfolio. As well, the increasing tax refund cheque he was getting each year allowed him to make extra payments against his mortgage to eliminate that bad debt very quickly, and this new equity was also instantly reborrowed to increase the portfolio yet again. As you can see from the chart above, Mark had eliminated the non-deductible mortgage loan in 22 years versus the original 25 years – the length of time Darren was making non-deductible mortgage payments.

No Debt Increase but a Significant Increase in Net Worth

Mark made these large improvements without leveraging in the traditional sense. Part of the risk in leveraging comes from the increased costs of carrying a higher amount of debt. *The Smith Manoeuvre* is not a 'leveraging' program because even though you will technically be borrowing to purchase investments, you will not have access to the funds unless first you reduce your mortgage by the amount you wish to borrow to invest. If you reduce your bad debt before you borrow back to invest, you have not leveraged, you have *converted*. The difference is important to understand.

In truth the leveraging occurred earlier when Mark borrowed $400,000 to buy his house. In fact, he fully leveraged into bad debt for a good purchase, his house. With *The Smith Manoeuvre* available for his use, Mark can now make a prior good decision (to leverage into a house) into a much better decision (to convert the bad debt into good debt).

Using *The Smith Manoeuvre*, Mark has managed to improve his net worth in dramatic fashion without increasing his debt, and without using any of his own cash flow. In fact, Mark has a new source of free cash flow. It is courtesy of the tax department when he claims the fruits of the conversion of bad debt to good debt – juicy tax refund cheques.

What Is the Comparison?

Let's now have a gander at the differences in the circumstances of Darren and Mark. What are the cold, hard facts? Well, Darren retired at age 65 mortgage-free, just as he had always planned. But because he had managed to save precisely zero dollars throughout the course of paying out his mortgage, he had to sign up for a reverse mortgage and start selling the house back to the bank. He was actually concerned that he may live too long and that by doing so the bank would take *all* of the house when he died and there would be nothing left for the kids.

Mark, on the other hand, also retired at age 65 – three years after he paid out the non-deductible mortgage loan – but he had a taxable nest egg valued at $840,394 on which he could rely for retirement income. While he did have an investment loan of $400,000 as well, if we look at the net position, he had the value of his house and the net value of his investment portfolio of $440,394 to enjoy ($840,394 taxable portfolio less $400,000 deductible investment loan). Figure 4.5 assumes straight-line appreciation of the respective homes from $500,000 at age 40 to $800,000 at age 80.

	Age								
Darren	**40**	**45**	**50**	**55**	**60**	**65**	**70**	**75**	**80**
Assets									
Investments	$0	$0	$0	$0	$0	$0	$0	$0	$0
House	$500,000	$537,500	$575,000	$612,500	$650,000	$687,500	$725,000	$762,500	$800,000
Total assets	$500,000	$537,500	$575,000	$612,500	$650,000	$687,500	$725,000	$762,500	$800,000
Liabilities									
Mortgage + Reverse Mortgage	$400,000	$348,216	$285,091	$208,142	$114,342	$290,000	$393,053	$532,727	$722,035
Net Worth	**$100,000**	**$189,284**	**$289,909**	**$404,358**	**$535,658**	**$397,500**	**$331,947**	**$229,773**	**$77,965**
Mark									
Assets									
Investments	$0	$59,386	$150,818	$292,639	$511,328	$840,394	$840,394	$840,394	$840,394
House	$500,000	$537,500	$575,000	$612,500	$650,000	$687,500	$725,000	$762,500	$800,000
Total assets	$500,000	$596,886	$725,818	$905,139	$1,161,328	$1,527,894	$1,565,394	$1,602,894	$1,640,394
Liabilities									
Mortgage + Investment Loan	$400,000	$400,000	$400,000	$400,000	$400,000	$400,000	$400,000	$400,000	$400,000
Net Worth	**$100,000**	**$196,886**	**$325,818**	**$505,139**	**$761,328**	**$1,127,894**	**$1,165,394**	**$1,202,894**	**$1,240,394**
Improvement in Mark's Net Worth vs Darren	**$0**	**$7,602**	**$35,909**	**$100,781**	**$225,670**	**$730,394**	**$833,447**	**$973,121**	**$1,162,429**

Fig. 4.5

So Mark had a net worth of $1,127,894 at age 65 and it just kept on growing. Darren, meanwhile, saw his net worth at age 65 at only $397,500. And it declined from there.

I hope the destructive nature of non-tax-deductible debt and the dangers of foregoing compound growth are becoming evident. The wealthy embrace tax-deductible debt and this allows them to embrace compound growth…and they measure wealth by net worth, not by how little debt they have. Darren was convinced all his working life that he had to eliminate his debt in order to increase his wealth and ended up with more non-deductible debt than he started with at age 40.

What Do Your Numbers Look Like?

You can download *The Smithman Calculator* at www.smithman.net and plug in your own assumptions as regards current or proposed mortgage balance, amortization, interest rates, your marginal tax rate and projected investment growth rates to see how your current non-*Smith Manoeuvre* plan compares to the result if you implemented *The Smith Manoeuvre* now.

Congratulations!

I just want to take a quick moment to congratulate you on reading this far. Just by getting to this point, you are way ahead of most Canadians and can even stop right now and still see enormous benefits by implementing the basic form of *The Smith Manoeuvre* as explained up to here…

…but if you want to speed up the elimination of the mortgage debt even faster, generate even more tax deductions, and build an even bigger nest egg, keep reading.

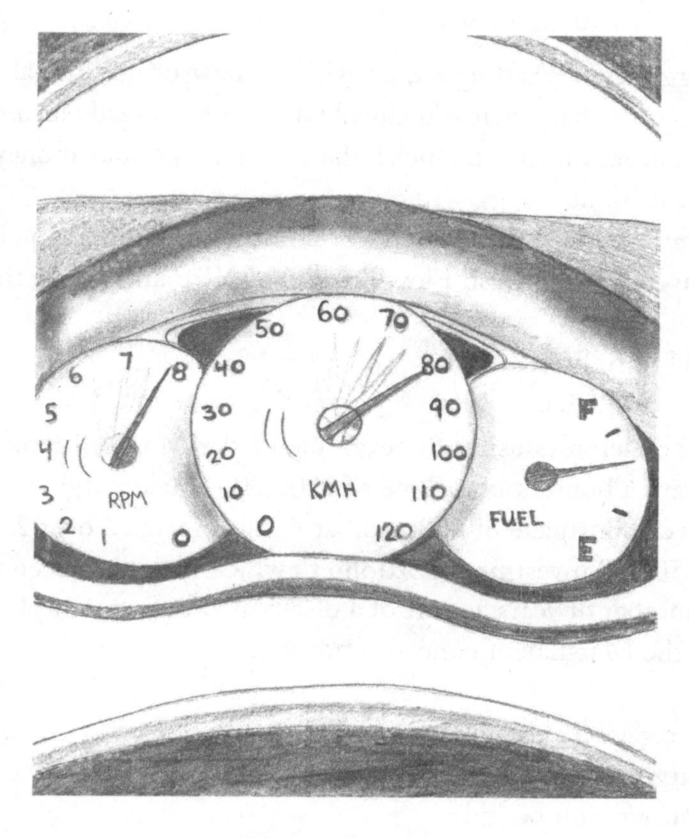

CHAPTER 5

ACCELERATORS

What we've just seen above is what we call the *Plain Jane Smith Manoeuvre*. Basically, this is simply taking the mortgage payment that you are already making anyways – nothing else – and putting it to work in order to create valuable tax deductions which lead to tax refunds allowing you to prepay the mortgage once a year at minimum and therefore being rid of that expensive, non-deductible mortgage debt much quicker than otherwise. And in order to generate those deductions you *must* invest, therefore improving your net worth on a monthly basis and building up retirement savings to allow you to avoid being forced to downsize or having to sell the house back to the bank in retirement.

All of this starts happening now. Not in 25 years, not next year, but now.

That being said, there are ways to speed the process up considerably – generate bigger tax deductions and refunds faster, eliminate the non-deductible mortgage debt faster, and build your nest egg faster. And again, all without new or additional money from you. Without anything more than what you already have or are already laying out each month. You just need to restructure your financial affairs and make your money work more than once. Really make it sweat.

We call them 'accelerators', and there are a number of them. Namely the Debt Swap, the Cash Flow Diversion, the Cash Flow Dam, the DRiP and Prime the Pump.

Let's Meet the Marshalls

Let's explore the accelerators using the example of the Marshall family. The Marshalls are 40 years old, have a household income of $100,000 and a marginal tax rate of 38.29%. They currently have a mortgage of $500,000 at 4.2% amortized over 25 years. Offsetting that liability is a $50,000 investment portfolio to which they have been contributing $500 per month for a number of years as part of a disciplined investment plan.

To summarize the Marshalls' financial condition:

$500,000	mortgage loan amount
38.29%	marginal tax rate
25 yrs.	amortization period
4.20%	interest rate of the mortgage
4.45%	interest rate of borrowing to invest
$100,000	total family gross income
8.0%	assumed annual average rate of return on investments
$500	monthly purchase of investments
$50,000	current value of accumulated investments

The Marshalls decide to consider implementing the *Plain Jane Smith Manoeuvre* (reborrow the monthly principal reduction of their mortgage to invest and apply the resultant annual tax refunds against the mortgage and get that invested too, as discussed in the previous chapter) and input their numbers into *The Smithman Calculator*.

By doing so they see that they are looking at having their non-deductible mortgage converted into a 100% tax-deductible investment loan in just over 22 years by the time they are 62 years old, and due to their retirement savings program allowed by *The Smith Manoeuvre*, have a net position of $545,798 ($1,045,798 minus the deductible investment loan of $500,000) as per figure 5.1. They decide to consult an accredited *Smith Manoeuvre*

Certified Professional mortgage broker and get that readvanceable mortgage they require to implement *The Smith Manoeuvre*.

The Two Steps of the *Plain Jane Smith Manoeuvre*:

Step I

Borrow back and invest the monthly principal reduction that occurs as you make your monthly mortgage payments over the months remaining on your mortgage. Borrowing the money back to invest creates an investment loan and the interest on this investment loan is tax-deductible.

Step II

Each year, when your tax refund arrives, use this money to make an extra payment against your mortgage, then immediately reborrow and invest the same amount.

That's it. That's all it takes to start the *Plain Jane Smith Manoeuvre* working for the Marshalls. As we see, pretty good results for simply restructuring their financial affairs at little to no cost to them at age 40.

COMPARATIVE STRATEGY SUMMARIES FOR THE MARSHALL FAMILY

A. The usual way - pay off the mortgage to zero while investing as much cash as possible for 25 years at 8%

		Debt		Tax		Time to	Net Worth after 25 Yrs.		
		Start	End	Deductions	Refunds	Conversion	Investments	Debt	Net Worth
Current Mortgage		$500,000	0	0	0	25.00 yrs	-	-	-
Current Savings -	$50,000	-	-	0	0	25.00 yrs	$367,009	$0	$367,009
Monthly Savings -	$500	-	-	0	0	25.00 yrs	$475,513	$0	$475,513
									$842,522

B. *The Smith Manoeuvre* way - convert the bad debt to good debt, reborrow to invest, generate tax deductions to apply against the mortgage to increase deductible borrowing for investments for 25 years at 8%.

	Start	End	Deductions	Refunds	Time to Conversion	Investments	Debt	Net Worth
After Step I	$500,000	$500,000	$229,876	$88,019	25.00 yrs	$873,120	$500,000	$373,120
After Step II	$500,000	$500,000	$258,764	$99,081	22.17 yrs	$1,045,798	$500,000	$545,798
								$545,798

Future value of the Marshall way ($842,522) **plus** *The Smith Manoeuvre* ($545,798 - Steps I and II)	**$1,388,320**
Future value of the Marshall way alone ($50,000 existing and $500/mo **with no** *Smith Manoeuvre*)	**$842,522**
Improvement in net worth due to *The Smith Manoeuvre* versus no *Smith Manoeuvre*	**$545,798**

C. Summary - assuming the same starting position for each strategy regarding debt, time, investment rate of return, monthly investment amounts and current investment values, *The Smith Manoeuvre* has increased the future value of the Marshall's net worth from $842,522 to $1,388,321. An increase of $545,798.

Fig. 5.1

We can see in figure 5.1 that the Marshalls were already on track to have their mortgage paid out in 25 years with a retirement portfolio valued at $842,522 due to the $50,000 in investments and monthly contribution of $500. That is the result they would have achieved had they not implemented *The Smith Manoeuvre*. Not bad.

But *The Smith Manoeuvre* – just steps one and two – sees their expensive non-deductible mortgage debt eliminated in 22 years, not 25 years, and their net position of $545,798 due solely to having implemented *The Plain Jane Smith Manoeuvre*, when added to their investment portfolio held outside *The Smith Manoeuvre*, sees their total net worth at $1,388,320 after 25 years. *The Smith Manoeuvre* added well over half a million dollars in net worth to the Marshalls over the course of 25 years – all for just making a decision and restructuring their finances when they were 40 years old.

But as we know, the Marshalls have been fortunate enough to have saved $50,000 in paid-up mutual funds. Is there a way to use this to increase the benefit of *The Smith Manoeuvre*?

1. Debt Swap Accelerator

While maybe not exactly the norm in these expensive times, it is not too much of a stretch to imagine that a family may have several thousand in savings. Yes, life is expensive, but every once in a while, we may be able to put a couple bucks aside and over time this adds up. The Marshalls have accrued $50,000 in paid-up mutual funds over the years so let's see how they can use this existing $50,000 in investments to drastically improve upon the *Plain Jane Smith Manoeuvre*, which itself was an impressive improvement versus concentrating on paying off the mortgage conventionally at the expense of *not* investing the newly created equity in their home each month for retirement.

All we need to do is instruct a redemption of these assets, get hold of the $50,000 in cash, make a prepayment of $50,000 against the non-deductible mortgage, and then, by nature of the readvanceable mortgage, reborrow it from the line of credit when it automatically increases its limit a few days later, and get invested again with the same $50,000. So what have we done?

Recall the Marshalls currently have an expensive, non-deductible $500,000 mortgage. After they apply the $50,000 in cash from the investment redemption and reborrow to invest again, they all of a sudden have $450,000 in non-deductible mortgage debt, $50,000 in deductible debt and the same $50,000 in investments. They have swapped $50,000 of non-deductible debt for $50,000 of deductible debt. And at their marginal tax rate of about 40%, that is immediately worth about $890 per year in tax refunds. Not bad at all.

Before Debt Swap					After Debt Swap				
Non-deductible Debt	Deductible Debt	Total Debt	Investment Assets	Tax Benefit	Non-deductible Debt	Deductible Debt	Total Debt	Investment Assets	Tax Benefit
$500,000	$0	**$500,000**	$50,000	**$0**	$450,000	$50,000	**$500,000**	$50,000	**$890**

Fig. 5.2

As figure 5.2 shows, compared to not executing a Debt Swap and having $500,000 in non-deductible debt and $50,000 in investments, this is a big improvement. And it all can be accomplished within a week to ten days or so.

Figure 5.3 is the same chart used previously which compares the Marshalls' position after steps one, two and three – the Debt Swap.

COMPARATIVE STRATEGY SUMMARIES FOR THE MARSHALL FAMILY

A. The usual way - pay off the mortgage to zero while investing as much cash as possible for 25 years at 8%

		Debt		Tax		Time to	Net Worth after 25 Yrs.		
		Start	End	Deductions	Refunds	Conversion	Investments	Debt	Net Worth
Current Mortgage		$500,000	0	0	0	25.00 yrs	-	-	-
Current Savings -	$50,000	-	-	0	0	25.00 yrs	$367,009	$0	$367,009
Monthly Savings -	$500	-	-	0	0	25.00 yrs	$475,513	$0	$475,513
									$842,522

B. The Marshall way after executing the $50,000 Debt Swap into *The Smith Manoeuvre*

Current Savings -	$0	-	-	0	0	25.00 yrs	$0	$0	$0
Monthly Savings -	$500	-	-	0	0	25.00 yrs	$475,513	$0	**$475,513**

C. *The Smith Manoeuvre* way - convert the bad debt to good debt, reborrow to invest, generate tax deductions to apply against the mortgage to increase deductible borrowing for investments for 25 years at 8%.

	Start	End	Deductions	Refunds	Conversion	Investments	Debt	Net Worth
After Step I	$500,000	$500,000	$229,876	$88,019	25.00 yrs	$873,120	$500,000	$373,120
After Step II	$500,000	$500,000	$258,764	$99,081	22.17 yrs	$1,045,798	$500,000	$545,798
After Step III	$500,000	$500,000	$341,410	$130,726	18.33 yrs	$1,485,021	$500,000	$985,021
								$985,021

Future value of the new Marshall way ($500/mo outside of *Smith Manoeuvre* - section B.)	**$475,513**
plus: future value of *The Smith Manoeuvre* (Steps I to III)	**$985,021**
Total net worth of Marshall family	**$1,460,534**
Improvement in net worth due to *The Smith Manoeuvre* (Steps I to III) versus no *Smith Manoeuvre* (section A.)	**$618,012**

D. Summary - assuming the same starting position for each strategy regarding debt, time, investment rate of return, monthly investment amounts and current investment values, *The Smith Manoeuvre* has increased the future value of the Marshall's net worth from $842,522 to $1,460,534. An increase of $618,012.

Fig. 5.3

This one transaction translates into being rid of that non-deductible mortgage in 18.33 years, increased tax deductions to over $341,000 over the life of the original amortization period, and added over $618,000 of net worth for a total of over $1.46 million. And all the Marshalls did to gain this improvement was sell their investment, transfer the cash through their mortgage and repurchase the investment.

The Marshalls are going to want to consult their investment advisor about the effect of taxation on the redemption of the investment and any transaction or commission costs, and they need to be aware of certain rules which govern against the sale and repurchase of identical investments within a certain timeframe, (namely the 'superficial loss rule' – more on this in *The Smith Manoeuvre Homeowner Course*) but the principle remains. And just so you're clear, the Debt Swap can be executed at any time – not just at refinance or when purchasing a new house. Fantastic, long-lasting benefit for one simple transaction that takes merely days.

> Step III The Debt Swap Accelerator
>
> Reduce your non-deductible mortgage balance using cash obtained by liquidating any available term deposits, CSBs, GICs, mutual funds, stocks and bonds or other non-registered paid-up assets you own, and then borrow back the same amount to invest in replacement assets. It should also be stated here that the Debt Swap can be done simply with any lump sum of cash you may have available – whether the cash comes from redeemed assets or from a chunk of change you were holding in cash for emergencies or from an inheritance. The Debt Swap is the act of swapping non-deductible debt for deductible debt using money regardless of the money's source.

I would like to note here that depending on the prepayment privileges of the existing mortgage they were looking to pay out and the prepayment privilege of the new readvanceable mortgage they were getting into, they may be better off selling the investments to prepay the existing mortgage just prior to refinance and then, with the lower mortgage balance on the new readvanceable mortgage, use the excess credit to reborrow the $50,000 to get back into investments. This is a determination for your *Smith Manoeuvre Certified Professional* advisor, however, but the effect is essentially the same.

2. Cash Flow Diversion Accelerator

But how did the Marshalls build up that $50,000 they just used for the Debt Swap in the first place? Well, they were in the fortunate position to be able to add $500 per month from personal cash flow to their investment portfolio for a goodly number of years. It is that $500 a month that grew to $50,000 over time. So is there a way to further utilize this monthly sum that they are saving anyways? To make that $500 sweat as well? Yes, and it is called the Cash Flow Diversion Accelerator. Again, no new money from these folks is required.

The Marshalls have been diligently outlaying $500 of personal cash flow to date each month in any event and they will continue to commit this amount to investments, as was always their plan, but we are going to get them to rearrange the way they get this invested in order to speed up the elimination of the mortgage, to turbocharge the generation of tax deductions and therefore the size of their tax refunds, all while getting that money invested that they already were anyways.

Good Advice, but It Could Have Been Better

To date the Marshalls have, on the good (but not perfect) advice of their planner, had a mutual fund company come directly into their bank account on the first day of each and every month and automatically take $500 to invest in one of the fund company's mutual funds. It was good advice because investing for the future is rarely bad advice, but it is imperfect advice because they should have been advised to make their money work more than once for them.

What we are going to get the Marshalls to do is simply request the fund company come into their bank account – their new *Smith Manoeuvre Chequing Account* used exclusively for their *Smith Manoeuvre* – a bit later into each month instead of the first. Simply shift the day they take that money to invest for them. Why? Because we just need a few extra days to first run that $500 through the mortgage.

At the beginning of each month the Marshalls are going to make a prepayment against their mortgage of $500 from their *Personal Chequing Account.* Depending from which lender they got their readvanceable mortgage, it is likely that all they have to do is go online, sign in, and request a $500 prepayment (or they could voluntarily increase their regular mortgage payment by $500). The mortgage lender is going to take that $500 and apply it against the mortgage balance – and every dollar of it is going to go against principal (which is to your benefit), none to interest (which would be to the bank's benefit).

So, if the Marshalls' regular mortgage payment was going to reduce $950 of principal, because they are prepaying by another $500, the principal reduction is actually $1,450 on that expensive mortgage. And the nature of the readvanceable mortgage means they are able to reborrow that full $1,450 into their *Smith Manoeuvre Chequing Account* for investment, not just $950 as per the *Plain Jane Smith Manoeuvre.* Figure 5.4 shows what their numbers now look like on the comparison chart:

COMPARATIVE STRATEGY SUMMARIES FOR THE MARSHALL FAMILY

A. The usual way - pay off the mortgage to zero while investing as much cash as possible for 25 years at 8%

		Debt		Tax		Time to	Net Worth after 25 Yrs.		
		Start	End	Deductions	Refunds	Conversion	Investments	Debt	Net Worth
Current Mortgage		$500,000	0	0	0	25.00 yrs	-	-	-
Current Savings -	$50,000	-	-	0	0	25.00 yrs	$367,009	$0	$367,009
Monthly Savings -	$500	-	-	0	0	25.00 yrs	$475,513	$0	$475,513
									$842,522

B. *The Smith Manoeuvre* way - convert the bad debt to good debt, reborrow to invest, generate tax deductions to apply against the mortgage to increase deductible borrowing for investments for 25 years at 8%.

	Start	End	Deductions	Refunds	Time to Conversion	Investments	Debt	Net Worth
After Step I	$500,000	$500,000	$229,876	$88,019	25.00 yrs	$873,120	$500,000	$373,120
After Step II	$500,000	$500,000	$258,764	$99,081	22.17 yrs	$1,045,798	$500,000	$545,798
After Step III	$500,000	$500,000	$341,410	$130,726	18.33 yrs	$1,485,021	$500,000	$985,021
After Step IV	$500,000	$500,000	$389,908	$149,296	14.50 yrs	$2,004,119	$500,000	$1,504,119
								$1,504,119

Future value of *The Smith Manoeuvre* (Steps I to IV)	**$1,504,119**
Future value of the Marshall way	**$842,522**
Improvement in net worth due to *The Smith Manoeuvre* (Steps I to IV) versus no *Smith Manoeuvre* (section A.)	**$661,597**

C. Summary - assuming the same starting position for each strategy regarding debt, time, investment rate of return, monthly investment amounts and current investment values, *The Smith Manoeuvre* has increased the future value of the Marshall's net worth from $842,522 to $1,504,119. An increase of $661,597.

Fig. 5.4

They are still getting that $500 invested each month that they were prior to redirecting it against the mortgage, so no new money out of their pockets, but the monthly prepayments and resultant increase in tax deductions means they are able to eliminate their non-deductible mortgage in 14.5 years. Better than the already impressive results from the *Plain Jane Smith Manoeuvre* plus Debt Swap and much, much better than the original 25 years by paying it off conventionally. In addition, their projected net worth after 25 years has increased to a very impressive $1,504,119.

We will discuss salvaged payments when consolidating non-deductible debt or preserving deductible debt a bit later, and when we do, I will remind you that this is where that would come in – diverting those previous payments through the mortgage to your benefit, saving in non-deductible interest expense, and converting the mortgage and building your retirement fund all the more quickly. But for the sake of comparison in this section, we will assume the Marshalls had no non-deductible debt to consolidate nor any deductible debt to preserve.

Step IV The Cash Flow Diversion Accelerator

Divert current monthly savings and investment plan amounts against the mortgage loan, and then borrow back the same amount to invest.

So can even this scenario with the Cash Flow Diversion of $500 per month in savings they were already putting away be improved upon for the Marshalls? Actually it can, because they happen to own a proprietorship. Maybe you do too?

3. Cash Flow Dam Accelerator

When most small businesses get started, part of the excitement is going to the bank to open a business account. You order company cheque books and deposit books. The money starts to flow in to your new bank account and at the end of the month you pay the company bills. If there is anything left, you write a cheque to yourself, call it a 'draw', and deposit it to your *Personal Chequing Account*.

If you don't have a house mortgage this is a fine and efficient setup. But if you do have a mortgage, then there is a much better way to structure your banking. It is called the Cash Flow Dam and it is extremely powerful.

The Marshalls' proprietorship – a rental property – is nothing too fancy, but a nice little place for which they have found good renters who pay on time every month and keep the house and garden tidy. The Marshalls receive $2,000 in rent each month from their tenants and promptly use it to pay the expenses, including the mortgage payment, on their rental property which also happens to total $2,000 per month. So the Marshalls are not really generating any extra cash flow from this little business they have, but house prices have been and continue to increase steadily and they will eventually sell the rental house and have a tidy sum left over after they pay out the remaining mortgage balance, if any, at that time.

However, the Marshalls, and likely thousands of other Canadians, have been making a very expensive mistake each and every month. They are receiving rental receipts each month and promptly redirecting them to cover the mortgage payment and other expenses on their investment property. Money in, money out. While this seems the appropriate thing to do – after all, they have a mortgage on their rental, and they have promised their bank to make payments on it each month – it is not. They are missing out on thousands and thousands of dollars of benefit.

Make Your Money Work More Than Once

Income from a proprietorship can be used as the owner sees fit. And so if the rental income you receive from your business is yours to do with as you like, let's make it really sweat. What the Marshalls should be doing is applying these rental receipts of $2,000 per month as a *prepayment* against the non-deductible mortgage of their *principal* residence – the mortgage on the house in which they live. Bam! – a monthly $2,000 *prepayment* of the mortgage, on top of the $500 per month Cash Flow Diversion and also the regular mortgage payment they were making anyways? They will see that non-deductible mortgage eliminated in record time. Extremely powerful.

But what about servicing the expenses and the mortgage payments on the rental property, you say? Well, you'll remember that as soon as you make a reduction in the mortgage balance of your principal residence, the line of credit increases its limit dollar-for-dollar. While the reductions caused by the regular mortgage payment and $500 Cash Flow Diversion, you'll recall, are reborrowed to *invest* in *securities* in order to accrue assets to pad the Marshalls' retirement fund, the $2,000 from the Cash Flow Dam principal reduction is reborrowed in order to *invest* in their *business* – the rental property.

When this $2,000 of the total amount available to reborrow from the line of credit is pulled out, it then, and only then, goes to pay their rental property expenses. This monthly $2,000 reborrowing from their line of credit does not pollute the purity of deductibility of the line of credit because they are still 'borrowing to invest'. Nothing in the Tax Act says that you have to pay business expenses directly with revenue generated by the unincorporated business. They are borrowing to invest in their business, and therefore the interest on that borrowing is tax-deductible. Boom! Up goes their tax deductions. Boom! Up goes their tax refunds they can also use as mortgage prepayments. Boom! Away goes that non-deductible mortgage debt. A $2,000 prepayment against their mortgage each and every month is very, very powerful.

Further, if your revenues are greater than the expenses of the proprietorship, then you are able to invest the difference each month to increase your investment portfolio. For example, if your revenues were $2,000 per month but the expenses total only $1,500, then after you prepay the mortgage loan by the full $2,000 and reborrow that full amount as well, there is $500 to invest in securities after you service the proprietorship expenses of $1,500.

Step V The Cash Flow Dam Accelerator

Use proprietorship revenues to prepay the mortgage loan, then reborrow to service the proprietorship expenses. If the revenues are greater than the expenses, invest the difference.

What Do We Have Going on so Far?

So at this point, while the $50,000 Debt Swap was a powerful *one-time event*, the Marshalls have *monthly principal reductions*, and therefore *monthly line of credit limit increases* from a few sources which they can get invested:

- The principal component of the regular monthly mortgage payment (invest into their investment portfolio)
- The $500 per month via the Cash Flow Diversion (invest into their investment portfolio)
- And now $2,000 via the Cash Flow Dam (invest into their rental business)

As we can see by figure 5.5, the results improved even more: over $467,000 in tax deductions, meaning the resultant increased tax refunds help eliminate the nón-deductible mortgage in only 8.17 years. The investment portfolio has increased to almost $2.1 million leading to a total net worth of just under $1.6 million. And don't forget, this excludes any increase in home equity the Marshalls may have enjoyed. The comparison here is net worth of $1.6 million due to implementing *The Smith Manoeuvre* as described to this point versus just over $842,500 if they had not. Almost double the dollars.

COMPARATIVE STRATEGY SUMMARIES FOR THE MARSHALL FAMILY

A. The usual way - pay off the mortgage to zero while investing as much cash as possible for 25 years at 8%

		Debt		Tax		Time to	Net Worth after 25 Yrs.		
		Start	End	Deductions	Refunds	Conversion	Investments	Debt	Net Worth
Current Mortgage		$500,000	0	0	0	25.00 yrs	-	-	-
Current Savings -	$50,000	-	-	0	0	25.00 yrs	$367,009	$0	$367,009
Monthly Savings -	$500	-	-	0	0	25.00 yrs	$475,513	$0	$475,513
									$842,522

B. *The Smith Manoeuvre* way - convert the bad debt to good debt, reborrow to invest, generate tax deductions to apply against the mortgage to increase deductible borrowing for investments for 25 years at 8%.

	Start	End	Deductions	Refunds	Time to Conversion	Investments	Debt	Net Worth
After Step I	$500,000	$500,000	$229,876	$88,019	25.00 yrs	$873,120	$500,000	$373,120
After Step II	$500,000	$500,000	$258,764	$99,081	22.17 yrs	$1,045,798	$500,000	$545,798
After Step III	$500,000	$500,000	$341,410	$130,726	18.33 yrs	$1,485,021	$500,000	$985,021
After Step IV	$500,000	$500,000	$389,908	$149,296	14.50 yrs	$2,004,119	$500,000	$1,504,119
After Step V	$500,000	$500,000	$467,468	$178,993	8.17 yrs	$2,094,946	$500,000	$1,594,946
								$1,594,946

Future value of *The Smith Manoeuvre* (Steps I to V)	**$1,594,946**
Future value of the Marshall way	**$842,522**
Improvement in net worth due to *The Smith Manoeuvre* (Steps I to V) versus no *Smith Manoeuvre* (section A.)	**$752,424**

C. Summary - assuming the same starting position for each strategy regarding debt, time, investment rate of return, monthly investment amounts and current investment values, *The Smith Manoeuvre* has increased the future value of the Marshall's net worth from $842,522 to $1,594,946. An increase of $752,424.

Fig. 5.5

Cash Flow Dam Summary

Being able to implement the Cash Flow Dam relies on you owning a proprietorship. A proprietorship is indeed a business but it is different than a corporation. A corporation is its own legal entity – you may own 100% of it but the corporation itself is as real as you are in the eyes of the law.

A proprietorship, however, is *you*. It is an unincorporated business that you run and own as if it were yourself. In other words, any income from the business is treated just the same as any income you receive in wages or salary from your job. And you can do anything you want with this income. Further, a proprietorship is not necessarily just a rental property, it can be a home-based business you own which sells pottery from the garage, a hotdog cart you roll out on weekends to the Friday night baseball game, etc. If the business is not incorporated, you can be reasonably certain that it is a proprietorship, but of course, and as always, check with your accountant.

If you expect to convert your proprietorship to a corporation at some future date, you will want to discuss this with an accountant. Also, you will want to be sure that bank accounts for your personal situation and any for the proprietorship are set up appropriately. So as there are a number of accounting and tax considerations when you are implementing the Cash Flow Dam, be sure to consult your financial and/or tax professional prior to setup to ensure proper record-keeping going forward. These important Cash Flow Dam issues are discussed in more detail in *The Smith Manoeuvre Homeowner Course*.

The Cash Flow Dam requires no new money and no new resources of any kind from the taxpayer. The benefits are free and accrue as a result of reorganizing your finances, just like wealthy people do.

4. The DRiP Accelerator

Betcha didn't think we could make this thing go even faster. Well, we can, and we call it the DRiP Accelerator.

Let's consider the fact that there are investments out there that can send you distributions – interest income, dividends, etc. – on a regular basis (monthly, quarterly, etc.). Typically, investors instruct these dividends to automatically reinvest in order to increase the number of 'units' or 'shares' of the investment they own through a DRiP program (Dividend ReInvestment Program). What if instead of these dividends automatically, immediately and directly reinvesting, say, each month, we instruct that they come to us in cash into our *Personal Chequing Account* each month? We can then take this new cash flow that otherwise we would not be seeing and apply it as a prepayment against our mortgage each month, and then pull it back out from the line of credit as per the monthly process already described in depth and get it invested.

If we had these dividends automatically reinvest each month we would be taking advantage of the magic of compound growth, but if we first take this new cash to prepay the mortgage and *then* get it invested, we still get to enjoy the magic of compound growth but first we put this cash to work accelerating the elimination of that expensive, non-deductible mortgage debt.

We're making those dividends work more than once – granted, at the beginning of the program the dividends are very, very small, but it won't take long for the dividends to compound to real money. For example, dividends on $8,000 of stock at 4% annually would be only $320 for the year, but when the portfolio is valued at, say $45,000, the dividends would be $1,800. And on a portfolio of $150,000, the dividends would be $6,000.

So, if the Marshalls were investing into an investment that generated 4% in dividends each year, here is what their program would now look like for them, remembering that with the Debt Swap, they have $50,000 invested to start:

COMPARATIVE STRATEGY SUMMARIES FOR THE MARSHALL FAMILY

A. The usual way - pay off the mortgage to zero while investing as much cash as possible for 25 years at 8%

		Debt		Tax		Time to	Net Worth after 25 Yrs.		
		Start	End	Deductions	Refunds	Conversion	Investments	Debt	Net Worth
Current Mortgage		$500,000	0	0	0	25.00 yrs	-	-	-
Current Savings -	$50,000	-	-	0	0	25.00 yrs	$367,009	$0	$367,009
Monthly Savings -	$500	-	-	0	0	25.00 yrs	$475,513	$0	$475,513
									$842,522

B. *The Smith Manoeuvre* way - convert the bad debt to good debt, reborrow to invest, generate tax deductions to apply against the mortgage to increase deductible borrowing for investments for 25 years at 8%.

	Debt Start	Debt End	Tax Deductions	Tax Refunds	Time to Conversion	Investments	Debt	Net Worth
After Step I	$500,000	$500,000	$229,876	$88,019	25.00 yrs	$873,120	$500,000	$373,120
After Step II	$500,000	$500,000	$258,764	$99,081	22.17 yrs	$1,045,798	$500,000	$545,798
After Step III	$500,000	$500,000	$341,410	$130,726	18.33 yrs	$1,485,021	$500,000	$985,021
After Step IV	$500,000	$500,000	$389,908	$149,296	14.50 yrs	$2,004,119	$500,000	$1,504,119
After Step V	$500,000	$500,000	$467,468	$178,993	8.17 yrs	$2,094,946	$500,000	$1,594,946
After Step VI	$500,000	$500,000	$473,919	$181,464	7.42 yrs	$2,103,658	$500,000	$1,603,658
								$1,603,658

Future value of *The Smith Manoeuvre* (Steps I to VI)	**$1,603,658**
Future value of the Marshall way	**$842,522**
Improvement in net worth due to *The Smith Manoeuvre* (Steps I to VI) versus no *Smith Manoeuvre* (section A.)	**$761,136**

C. Summary - assuming the same starting position for each strategy regarding debt, time, investment rate of return, monthly investment amounts and current investment values, *The Smith Manoeuvre* has increased the future value of the Marshall's net worth from $842,522 to $1,603,658. An increase of $761,136.

Fig. 5.6

We can see in figure 5.6 that this simple instruction of having the dividends sent to them in cash rather than immediately reinvesting them reduces the conversion period from 8.17 years as per the last example to 7.42 years, and their net worth increased just under $9,000 compared to the previous scenario. Bear in mind that while the increase in the portfolio value seems relatively small, we can't forget that these dividends would be invested either way – either before being run through the mortgage or after – but nine grand is nine grand and it didn't come from the Marshalls' pockets. Not one penny.

However, where the increase in portfolio value does come from is the fact that they are prepaying by more and more each subsequent period considering the increasing dividends they are receiving in cash, and this leads to increased tax refunds which can be used as prepayments and subsequently invested.

Step VI The DRiP Accelerator

Request dividends to be sent to you in cash rather than reinvested automatically. Use these dividends to prepay the mortgage loan, then reborrow to purchase the same stock or investment that issued the dividends or invest elsewhere.

5. Prime the Pump Accelerator

I would like to now discuss another way to boost the speed at which your investments and tax deductions can grow, and we call it Priming the Pump. You may recognize the saying as it relates to giving a little pump of the plastic bubble to inject a bit of extra fuel into the lawnmower's carburetor when starting it up for the first time in a while. It just gives it a little boost of juice to get it going.

In all of the above examples, we have been making the calculations based on a $500,000 mortgage for the Marshalls. But what we have not mentioned yet is the value of their house. When the Marshalls decided to implement *The Smith Manoeuvre*, they consulted a *Smith Manoeuvre Certified Professional* mortgage broker and refinanced into a readvanceable mortgage for $500,000. But what did their house appraise at? If it appraised at $625,000 then they would have qualified for a total loan from the mortgage lender for that $500,000, but no more, meaning they did not have any additional borrowing power beyond that half million dollars. Recall a readvanceable mortgage will only be extended to 80% of the appraised value of the house ($625,000 * 0.8 = $500,000). Figure 5.7 shows what their mortgage would have looked like at that $625,000 appraisal value:

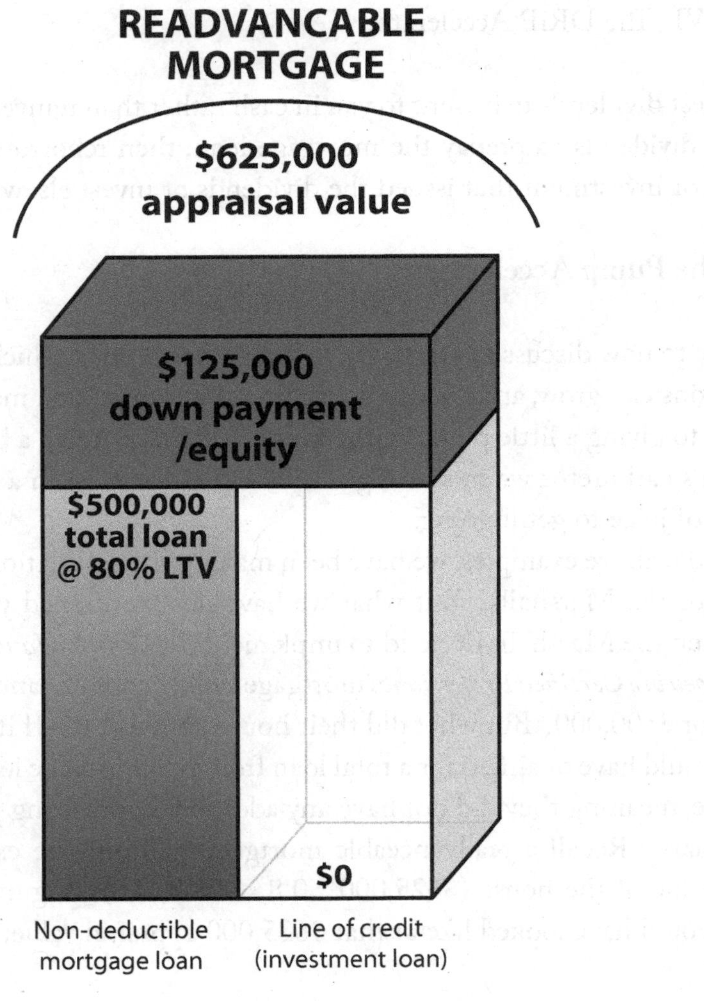

Fig. 5.7

They would have no additional borrowing power at refinance because the non-deductible mortgage of $500,000 they already had prior to refinance fully absorbs all the borrowing power of the new readvanceable mortgage. Therefore, the attached secured line of credit component starts out with a zero-dollar limit. Only when the non-deductible loan portion is reduced via the regular mortgage payment or any prepayments will the limit on the line of credit increase dollar for dollar and allow the Marshalls to pull it out to invest.

Maybe You Have More Than 20% Equity in Your House?

But what if their house actually appraised at $700,000 and the bank believed they were good for the full 80% total loan available? Well then, 80% of $700,000 works out to $560,000. So, what does their readvanceable mortgage look like at refinance in this case?

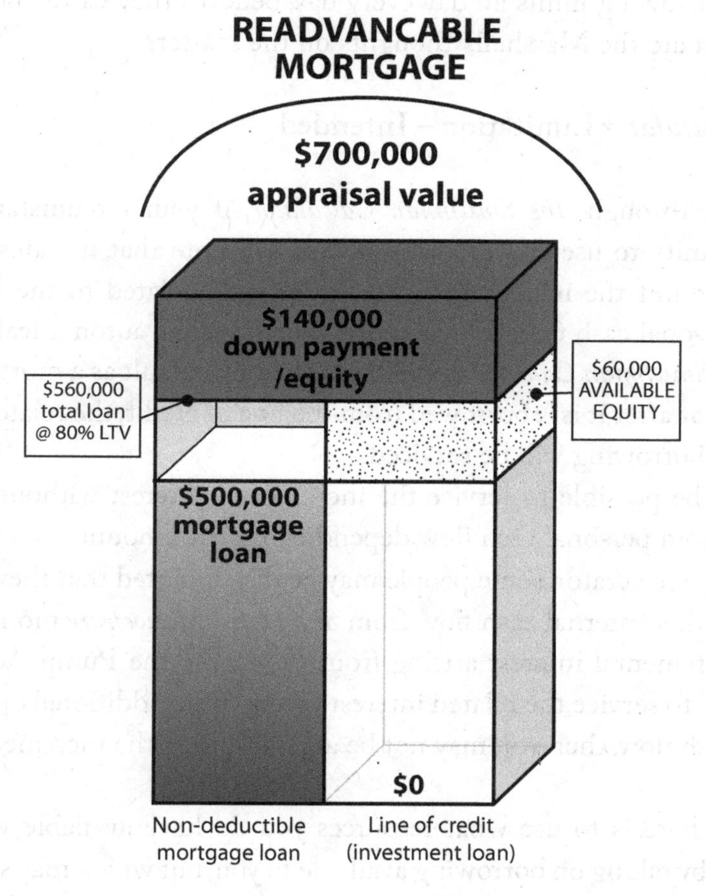

Fig. 5.8

What figure 5.8 is telling us is that while they still have $500,000 of non-deductible debt on the left side of the graphic that they need to convert to a deductible investment loan as quickly as possible, they also have a line of credit with an immediately available limit of $60,000 because the bank was willing to lend them a total of $560,000 right off the bat.

At this point the Marshalls have a decision to make – should they borrow none, or some, or all of that available credit to invest right away? To 'Prime the Pump', if you will. By Priming the Pump, the Marshalls would be taking on additional debt. And by doing so they would be taking on additional risk.

This is a decision that the Marshalls, along with their *Smith Manoeuvre Certified Professional* advisor, will make. What is their comfort level? While the bank, who assesses credit risk and borrowing limits all day every day, believes they can handle the total loan of $560,000, what are the Marshalls' thoughts on the matter?

A *Smithman Calculator* Limitation – Intended

When you work through *The Smithman Calculator*, if your circumstances present you with the opportunity to use this accelerator, you will note that it states the homeowner is required to commit the incremental interest expense related to the Prime the Pump amount from personal cash flow. The amount, which will be automatically calculated and indicated by *The Smithman Calculator*, will be applied by default as a mortgage prepayment each month so that after it is reborrowed from the line of credit, the related interest on this new discretional borrowing will be serviced.

While it may be possible to service the incremental interest without coming up with additional cash from personal cash flow depending on the amount you elect to use for the Prime the Pump Accelerator, some people may be disappointed that they cannot calculate the results as if other internal cash flow from *The Smith Manoeuvre* monthly process were servicing the incremental interest arising from the Prime the Pump Accelerator. But if you cannot afford to service the related interest arising from additional optional borrowing from personal cash flow, then you may not be able to 'afford' the incremental borrowing in the first place.

The objective here is to use what resources you do have available wisely, not spread yourself too thin by taking on borrowing available to you, but which may squeeze you. Plus, coming up with extra personal cash flow to cover the incremental interest will also greatly increase the speed of conversion and the growth of your *Personal Pension Plan*. Again, do not implement the Prime the Pump Accelerator without discussing this thoroughly with your *Smith Manoeuvre Certified Professional* advisor.

Back to the Marshalls…

For the purposes of demonstration, we will assume the Marshalls wish to pull the full

$60,000 to Prime the Pump. They are both gainfully employed, their future is looking bright, and they have crunched the numbers with their advisor. Plus, the bank was willing to lend them the full $560,000 and, the Marshalls reasoned, if they were buying their first house and they had an offer of a $560,000 total loan to allow them to purchase a house, they would likely not hesitate in accepting the full amount – and all of it non-deductible at that. So, after consultation with their advisor, they decided to get it invested as soon as they acquired that new readvanceable mortgage. What is the effect of that decision?

How Does It Help to Prime the Pump?

The Marshalls have $500,000 of non-deductible debt the day they refinance that they need to convert over time, but they now also have $60,000 immediately and directly invested for their retirement. In addition, they also complete the $50,000 Debt Swap previously discussed. So, within days of refinance they now have $110,000 invested in total, only $450,000 of non-deductible mortgage debt, and $110,000 of valuable tax-deductible debt. Not bad.

While this $60,000 investment day one does not *directly* help in speeding up the conversion of their mortgage because they cannot first borrow it out from the line of credit to prepay the mortgage then borrow it back again to invest (see Common Mistakes below), it does *indirectly* do them plenty of good because they have just generated a significant amount of tax deductions right off the bat. These increased tax deductions lead to a bigger tax refund at the end of year one (and every subsequent year) than they otherwise would have received from the tax department, and therefore they immediately start to have more money each year after that refund cheque arrives with which to prepay their non-deductible mortgage. And the more you prepay the mortgage, the faster it disintegrates.

It also speeds up the accrual of retirement assets firstly by having a big chunk of funds being invested for as long as possible – starting right away – and therefore enjoying the magic of compound growth for as long a time as possible; but secondly, those bigger tax refunds that started to arrive to help to speed up the conversion? They also help in the accrual of investments because when we prepay the mortgage by that bigger once-a-year tax refund, there is more available to reborrow to invest. Starting year one and every subsequent year. Figure 5.9 again shows the comparison chart with the increased financial advantage from Priming the Pump.

COMPARATIVE STRATEGY SUMMARIES FOR THE MARSHALL FAMILY

A. The usual way - pay off the mortgage to zero while investing as much cash as possible for 25 years at 8%

		Debt		Tax		Time to	Net Worth after 25 Yrs.		
		Start	End	Deductions	Refunds	Conversion	Investments	Debt	Net Worth
Current Mortgage		$500,000	0	0	0	25.00 yrs	-	-	-
Current Savings -	$50,000	-	-	0	0	25.00 yrs	$367,009	$0	$367,009
Monthly Savings -	$500	-	-	0	0	25.00 yrs	$475,513	$0	$475,513
									$842,522

B. *The Smith Manoeuvre* way - convert the bad debt to good debt, reborrow to invest, generate tax deductions to apply against the mortgage to increase deductible borrowing for investments for 25 years at 8%.

	Start	End	Deductions	Refunds	Conversion	Investments	Debt	Net Worth
After Step I	$500,000	$500,000	$229,876	$88,019	25.00 yrs	$873,120	$500,000	$373,120
After Step II	$500,000	$500,000	$258,764	$99,081	22.17 yrs	$1,045,798	$500,000	$545,798
After Step III	$500,000	$500,000	$341,410	$130,726	18.33 yrs	$1,485,021	$500,000	$985,021
After Step IV	$500,000	$500,000	$390,507	$156,203	14.50 yrs	$2,019,057	$500,000	$1,519,057
After Step V	$500,000	$500,000	$467,468	$178,993	8.17 yrs	$2,094,946	$500,000	$1,594,946
After Step VI	$500,000	$500,000	$473,919	$181,464	7.42 yrs	$2,103,658	$500,000	$1,603,658
After Step VII	$560,000	$560,000	$547,920	$209,799	6.75 yrs	$2,627,033	$560,000	$2,067,033
								$2,067,033

Future value of *The Smith Manoeuvre* (Steps I to VII)	**$2,067,033**
Future value of the Marshall way	**$842,522**
Improvement in net worth due to *The Smith Manoeuvre* (Steps I to VII) versus no *Smith Manoeuvre* (section A.)	**$1,224,511**

C. Summary - assuming the same starting position for each strategy regarding debt, time, investment rate of return, monthly investment amounts and current investment values, *The Smith Manoeuvre* has increased the future value of the Marshall's net worth from $842,522 to $2,067,033. An increase of $1,224,511.

Fig. 5.9

Step VII The Prime the Pump Accelerator

If you have available funds that can be accessed immediately upon refinance into a readvanceable mortgage (or after restructuring your existing readvanceable mortgage), after a thorough discussion with your accredited *Smith Manoeuvre Certified Professional* advisor, you can directly invest some or all of the available funds. As this is discretionary borrowing, homeowners are advised to cover the incremental interest from personal cash flow and prepay the mortgage, then reborrow to service the related incremental deductible interest.

Let's Quantify

So we can see from this example that the time to the Marshalls' mortgage conversion has reduced from the previous example's 7.42 years down to 6.75 years. Their tax benefits over the 25 years have improved to $548,000 and their net worth has increased a cool $463,375 to a total of $2,067,033 simply due to Priming the Pump.

Wait a minute...I just had an idea. Would the Marshalls be able to pull that $60,000 and use it as a down payment for a second rental property to double the power of their existing Cash Flow Dam with two rental incomes to prepay the mortgage each month instead of one? Hmm....

Or for that matter, would you be able to use that for your own purchase of your *first* rental property in order to implement the Cash Flow Dam...? Something to consider down the road?

Did the Marshalls Manage to Keep up with the Joneses?

The Marshalls have same-aged neighbours to their east who have done pretty well for themselves. In fact, when the Marshalls decided to implement *The Smith Manoeuvre*, the Joneses were already making significantly more on an annual basis and had quite a bit more investments socked away already with more being purchased each month. Well, the Joneses were told about *The Smith Manoeuvre* by the Marshalls one night while sitting around the barbecue pit enjoying a bottle or two of Red Truck. However, they were not that keen to look into the strategy because they didn't really understand the difference between bad debt and good debt. Debt is debt, is it not? And so, they decided to continue on the well-worn path that most Canadians have been travelling. The path that, for many, leads to insufficient retirement savings, living off a fixed income, forced downsizing, a reverse mortgage, being supported by their children, etc.

Here's the Joneses' financial situation:

$500,000	mortgage loan amount
49.8%	marginal tax rate
25 yrs.	amortization period
4.2%	interest rate of the mortgage
$300,000	total family gross income
$700	monthly purchase of investments (Cash Flow Diversion)
$150,000	current value of accumulated investments (Debt Swap)
$48,000	annual rental receipts
$48,000	annual rental expenses

Compared to the Marshalls, the Joneses have identical mortgage terms but make $200,000 more per year, have $100,000 more in accrued investments and are contributing $700 per month to that, whereas the Marshalls are only contributing $500 a month to their investments.

Figure 5.10 is the chart comparing the future net worth of the Joneses' investment program without implementing *The Smith Manoeuvre* to the Marshalls' *Smith Manoeuvre* results.

COMPARATIVE STRATEGY SUMMARIES FOR THE MARSHALL FAMILY vs THE JONES FAMILY

A. The Jones's way - pay off the mortgage to zero while investing as much cash as possible for 25 years at 8%

		Debt		Tax		Time to	Net Worth after 25 Yrs.		
		Start	End	Deductions	Refunds	Conversion	Investments	Debt	Net Worth
Current Mortgage		$500,000	0	0	0	25.00 yrs	-	-	-
Current Savings -	$150,000	-	-	0	0	25.00 yrs	$1,101,026	$0	$1,101,026
Monthly Savings -	$700	-	-	0	0	25.00 yrs	$665,718	$0	$665,718
									$1,766,744

B. *The Smith Manoeuvre* way - convert the bad debt to good debt, reborrow to invest, generate tax deductions to apply against the mortgage to increase deductible borrowing for investments for 25 years at 8%.

	Start	End	Deductions	Refunds	Time to Conversion	Investments	Debt	Net Worth
After all Steps (I to VII)	$560,000	$560,000	$547,920	$209,799	6.75 yrs	$2,627,033	$560,000	**$2,067,033**

Future net worth of the Marshalls using *The Smith Manoeuvre*	**$2,067,033**
Future net worth of the Jones' (no *Smith Manoeuvre*)	**$1,766,744**
Improvement in the Marshall's net worth over the Jones's net worth	**$300,289**

C. Summary - assuming the same starting position for each strategy regarding debt, time, investment rate of return, monthly investment amounts and current investment values, the Marshall's projected net worth due to *The Smith Manoeuvre is* $2,067,033 versus the Jones' s projected net worth of $1,766,744. This represents an improvement of $300,289.

Fig. 5.10

The Joneses Aren't Necessarily in the Poor House but the Marshalls Are Way Better Off

The Joneses ended up coming out of this pretty good at retirement at age 65. They had their house clear title and $1,766,744 of retirement savings. Not bad.

The Marshalls, on the other hand, will have done significantly better due to a simple rearrangement of their financial affairs way back at 40 years old. All they did was speak with knowledgeable financial professionals and continue on with their existing financial plan, albeit with a twist: they refinanced into a readvanceable mortgage, executed the Debt Swap with $50,000 of existing investments, Primed the Pump with $60,000 of newly available credit due to the refinance, diverted their $500 in monthly savings and $2,000 in rental receipts to first go toward a mortgage prepayment each month, then reborrowed those sums, along with the principal reduction from the regular mortgage payment they were making in any event, in order to religiously invest each month into securities and their own business.

So what is the comparison here? At age 40, the Joneses were already significantly better off than the Marshalls – they had more, they made more, they invested more, and they continued to do so. Yet when age 65 rolled around, only 25 years later, their investment portfolio was a staggering $300,000 less than the Marshalls' portfolio.

What About a Lower Income Family?

Dan and Nancy Martin are in their early 30s, deeply in love and freshly married – haven't even gotten into their first fight yet...so sweet... They have just bought a small starter condo in Winnipeg where they are both working for start-ups. Below is their current condition and the results of doing it their way – no *Smith Manoeuvre* versus if they do implement *The Smith Manoeuvre*:

$200,000	mortgage loan amount
28.2%	marginal tax rate
25 yrs.	amortization period
5.0%	interest rate of the mortgage
4.45%	interest rate of borrowing to invest
$60,000	total family gross income
8.0%	assumed annual average rate of return on investments
$50	monthly purchase of investments (Cash Flow Diversion)
$5,000	current value of accumulated investments (Debt Swap)
4.0%	annual dividend yield for DRiP Accelerator

We can see by the chart in figure 5.11 that using *The Smith Manoeuvre* they were able to eliminate their non-deductible mortgage in only 16 years compared to 25 and there is a significant improvement in net worth for the Martin family even though they did not have as much ability to take advantage of the accelerators – in this case, they executed only the Debt Swap ($5,000), the Cash Flow Diversion ($50/month) and the DRiP (at 4% dividend yield) accelerators.

COMPARATIVE STRATEGY SUMMARIES FOR THE MARTIN FAMILY

A. The usual way - pay off the mortgage to zero while investing as much cash as possible for 25 years at 8%

		Debt		Tax		Time to	Net Worth after 25 Yrs.		
		Start	End	Deductions	Refunds	Conversion	Investments	Debt	Net Worth
Current Mortgage		$200,000	0	0	0	25.00 yrs	-	-	-
Current Savings -	$5,000	-	-	0	0	25.00 yrs	$36,701	$0	$36,701
Monthly Savings -	$50	-	-	0	0	25.00 yrs	$47,551	$0	$47,551
									$84,252

B. *The Smith Manoeuvre* way - convert the bad debt to good debt, reborrow to invest, generate tax deductions to apply against the mortgage to increase deductible borrowing for investments for 25 years at 8%.

	Start	End	Deductions	Refunds	Time to Conversion	Investments	Debt	Net Worth
After all available Steps	$200,000	$200,000	$136,206	$38,410	16.00 yrs	$512,589	$200,000	$312,589
								$312,589

Improvement in net worth due to *The Smith Manoeuvre* versus no *Smith Manoeuvre* (section A.) **$228,337**

C. Summary - assuming the same starting position for each strategy regarding debt, time, investment rate of return, monthly investment amounts and current investment values, *The Smith Manoeuvre* has increased the future value of the Martin's net worth from $84,252 to $312,589. An increase of $228,337.

Fig. 5.11

While the results may not seem as juicy as those of the Marshall family, consider this: the Martins are quite young, and chances are they will start to make more income with which they can increase their current $50 per month Cash Flow Diversion. Also, we can expect their house will increase in value and they will, at some point not too far off, be able to pull some additional equity out if they wish to Prime the Pump. And if they decide to have a family, they will upgrade their house and *The Smith Manoeuvre* process will begin to increase their net worth even faster. They might look more like the Marshalls pretty quickly.

What About a Higher Income Family?

What about a family that was in an even better financial position than the Marshalls upon starting their *Smith Manoeuvre*? Merv and Mel Petersen are in their mid-40s and own a construction and renovation firm just outside of Toronto. They also have a profitable rental property that they operate as a proprietorship. They have always been too busy to have any children (which may be why they've done so well…) but absolutely adore their Chihuahua. Merv has frequently been heard telling anyone who will listen, that "it takes a big man to walk a small dog." Here's the current condition and results for the Petersens:

$700,000	mortgage loan amount
49.8%	marginal tax rate
25 yrs.	amortization period
4.5%	interest rate of the mortgage
4.45%	interest rate of borrowing to invest
$300,000	total family gross income
8.0%	assumed annual average rate of return on investments
$1,500	monthly purchase of investments (Cash Flow Diversion)
$100,000	current value of accumulated investments (Debt Swap)
$85,000	amount used for Prime the Pump Accelerator
$3,500	monthly rental property revenues for Cash Flow Dam Accelerator
$2,000	monthly rental property expenses for Cash Flow Dam Accelerator
4%	annual dividend yield for DRiP Accelerator

COMPARATIVE STRATEGY SUMMARIES FOR THE PETERSEN FAMILY

A. The usual way - pay off the mortgage to zero while investing as much cash as possible for 25 years at 8%

		Debt		Tax		Time to	Net Worth after 25 Yrs.		
		Start	End	Deductions	Refunds	Conversion	Investments	Debt	Net Worth
Current Mortgage		$700,000	0	0	0	25.00 yrs	-	-	-
Current Savings -	$100,000	-	-	0	0	25.00 yrs	$734,018	$0	$734,018
Monthly Savings -	$1,500	-	-	0	0	25.00 yrs	$1,426,540	$0	$1,426,540
									$2,160,558

B. *The Smith Manoeuvre* way - convert the bad debt to good debt, reborrow to invest, generate tax deductions to apply against the mortgage to increase deductible borrowing for investments for 25 years at 8%.

	Start	End	Deductions	Refunds	Conversion	Investments	Debt	Net Worth
After all available Steps	$785,000	$785,000	$796,730	$396,772	5.08 yrs	$6,455,254	$785,000	$5,670,254
								$5,670,254

Improvement in net worth due to *The Smith Manoeuvre* versus no *Smith Manoeuvre* (section A.) **$3,509,696**

C. Summary - assuming the same starting position for each strategy regarding debt, time, investment rate of return, monthly investment amounts and current investment values, *The Smith Manoeuvre* has increased the future value of the Petersen's net worth from $2,160,558 to $5,670,254. An increase of $3,509,696.

Fig. 5.12

As we can see in figure 5.12, the Petersen family, by implementing *The Smith Manoeuvre*, will enjoy tax deductions of almost $800,000, tax refunds of almost $400,000, will have fully converted their mortgage in only five years as opposed to the original 25, and will have an investment portfolio valued at almost $6.5 million for a net worth of $5.67 million. This represents an improvement of over $3.5 million dollars compared to not implementing the strategy. In fact, even if the Petersens only earned 2% on their investment portfolio, they would still be better off with *The Smith Manoeuvre* by over $912,000.

What About an Older Family?

Before you assume that *The Smith Manoeuvre* is only for the younger crowd, let's look at Jerry and Trina Larsen. They've had a quiet but comfortable life and are now retired just outside Kelowna. Jerry was a golf pro before he retired (still can't hit a sand wedge) and both he and Trina, a former government employee, are fortunate enough to receive small but mostly sufficient pensions from their former employers. Here's what it looks like for the Larsens, who have only nine more years remaining on their mortgage:

$180,000	mortgage loan amount
28.2%	marginal tax rate
9 yrs.	amortization period
5.0%	interest rate of the mortgage
4.45%	interest rate of borrowing to invest
$75,000	total family gross income
8.0%	assumed annual average rate of return on investments
$300	monthly purchase of investments (Cash Flow Diversion)
$10,000	current value of accumulated investments (Debt Swap)
4.0%	annual dividend yield for DRiP Accelerator

As we can see in figure 5.13, they will require only 6.08 years to have paid out their non-deductible mortgage debt completely, and over the course of nine years – their remaining amortization period when they commenced *The Smith Manoeuvre* – they will have increased their net worth to almost $117,000. Compared to continuing with their conventional mortgage paydown and investment program, *The Smith Manoeuvre* has improved their net worth by over $49,000 in just nine years. And this near-$50,000 improvement did not cost them any extra monthly outlay of cash. No reduction in quality of life. In fact, the Larsens could still earn less than 3% on their investment portfolio and still come out significantly ahead of their original plan.

COMPARATIVE STRATEGY SUMMARIES FOR THE LARSEN FAMILY

A. The usual way - pay off the mortgage to zero while investing as much cash as possible for 9 years at 8%

		Debt		Tax		Time to	Net Worth after 25 Yrs.		
		Start	End	Deductions	Refunds	Conversion	Investments	Debt	Net Worth
Current Mortgage		$180,000	0	0	0	9.00 yrs	-	-	-
Current Savings -	$10,000	-	-	0	0	9.00 yrs	$20,495	$0	$20,495
Monthly Savings -	$300	-	-	0	0	9.00 yrs	$47,229	$0	$47,229
									$67,724

B. *The Smith Manoeuvre* way - convert the bad debt to good debt, reborrow to invest, generate tax deductions to apply against the mortgage to increase deductible borrowing for investments for 25 years at 8%.

	Start	End	Deductions	Refunds	Time to Conversion	Investments	Debt	Net Worth
After all available Steps	$180,000	$180,000	$46,208	$13,031	6.08 yrs	$296,771	$180,000	$116,771
								$116,771

Improvement in net worth due to *The Smith Manoeuvre* versus no *Smith Manoeuvre* (section A.) **$49,047**

C. Summary - assuming the same starting position for each strategy regarding debt, time, investment rate of return, monthly investment amounts and current investment values, *The Smith Manoeuvre* has increased the future value of the Larsen's net worth from $67,724 to $116,771. An increase of $49,047.

Fig. 5.13

The Smithman Calculator – available at www.smithman.net – will allow you input any or all of the above accelerators into your base-case condition to show you how you can improve your situation depending on your family's current and future realities. By using *The Smithman Calculator* there will be no guessing on your part as to how *The Smith Manoeuvre* can improve your family's financial circumstance. You can even experiment with relatively high interest rates and low forecasted investment returns to discover where your breakeven point is. You'll be pleasantly surprised at how high the interest rates and how low the forecasted growth rates can be with you still coming out ahead.

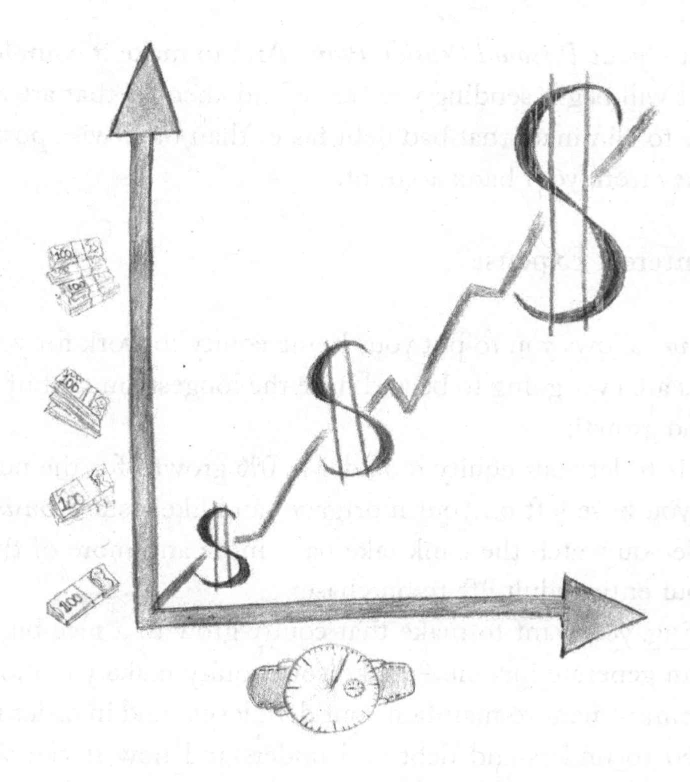

CHAPTER 6

LET'S TALK ABOUT DEBT AND WEALTH ACCUMULATION

Levels of Debt

The Smith Manoeuvre makes no recommendation on debt levels for the citizen. The strategy begins with the assumption that you and the bank are satisfied that you can handle the amount of leverage you have assumed in the mortgage loan you have already agreed to service before you read this book. You have already taken on the debt in the form of a mortgage which means you have already leveraged your borrowing power.

Whether you have too much or too little debt is between you and your accredited *Smith Manoeuvre Certified Professionals*. We know with certainty that because it's your house mortgage, the interest expense is not tax-deductible. *The Smith Manoeuvre* will fix that problem. Without increasing your debt, you have learned how to convert your bad loan to a good loan. Simultaneously you will start building a free-and-clear investment portfolio for your retirement – your *Personal Pension Plan*. And to make it completely worthwhile, the tax department will begin sending you tax refund cheques that are also tax-free with which you are able to eliminate that bad debt faster than otherwise possible. All of this, using no new money from your bank account.

A Bit More on Interest Expense

The Smith Manoeuvre allows you to put your home equity to work for you *now*, while you are as young as you are ever going to be and have the longest amount of time to enjoy the magic of compound growth.

The alternative is to let your equity moulder at 0% growth for the next 10-30 years or so (however long you have left on your mortgage) and likely start *consuming* your equity in retirement while you watch the bank take back more and more of the house that you worked so hard your entire adult life to purchase.

Instead of waiting, you want to make that equity grow to a nice big chunk of money with which you can generate income – make your equity make you money starting now. But it requires a commitment to maintain your debt levels, and in order to be comfortable with that you need to understand debt and understand how it can work for you, not against you.

In the United States, a good deal of mortgage loan interest paid by a taxpayer may be deducted from other income at tax-filing time and this can generate a tax refund cheque to the favour of the American taxpayer.

Things Are Different in Canada

In Canada, the tax department is not so generous. Interest paid on money borrowed to buy the family car, vacations, cottages, credit card consolidation and 'general consumption' cannot be deducted from other income for purposes of calculating income tax.

More importantly, interest on the largest loan many Canadians will ever take out, their house mortgage, is also not tax-deductible. No tax refund cheque there for the Canadian taxpayer. This is a huge disadvantage to Canadians. The fact that our American friends can deduct most of their mortgage interest when we can't goes some distance to explain why their standard of living tends to be higher than ours in Canada. You, as a Canadian, may claim no tax deduction. Unless you know how to do *The Smith Manoeuvre*.

To be fair, it should be pointed out that in Canada, we enjoy tax-free capital gains if we make a profit when we sell our home. In the States, a portion of the capital gains that might occur upon sale of the principal residence is taxed.

However, if you employ *The Smith Manoeuvre*, you will have the benefit of deductible interest *as well as* no capital gains tax upon the sale of your home: the best tax advantages of both countries. Suddenly, Canadians utilizing *The Smith Manoeuvre* will have even larger financial advantages than their American cousins.

When Can You Deduct Interest?

The Canada Revenue Agency (CRA) is very strict about claims for deductibility of interest. This item bears repeating. The basic test for deductibility revolves around the answer to the question *'to what purpose did you put the money that you borrowed?'* If you borrowed to buy the family car, to take a vacation, to buy a cottage or your principal residence, then you *may not* claim the interest on the loan as a tax deduction. On the other hand, if you borrowed the money to invest with a reasonable expectation of earning income from your investment, you *may* deduct the interest.

Interest and dividends from investments are acceptable forms of income for purposes of determining deductible interest claims, but capital gains are not. This is not to say you cannot enjoy capital gains in your portfolio without jeopardizing tax deductibility; it's to say that if you borrow to 'invest' in property which *only* generates capital gains, no expectation of income, then deductibility is jeopardized. In the case of borrowing to invest in mutual funds and stock, the CRA allows the interest to be deductible even in the cases where a portion of the gain is likely to be capital gains because there is *potential* for other types of income. Your *Smith Manoeuvre Certified Professional* financial planner or your accountant will counsel you on this matter if he or she feels you are exposed in any way.

Lastly, it is important to mention that any borrowing for *The Smith Manoeuvre* strategy be invested in a non-registered account. If this and the above-mentioned criteria are satisfied, then you can deduct the interest from your income. However, if you were to borrow to invest in registered investments (RRSPs, TFSAs, etc.) then the interest on the borrowing is not tax-deductible. This is because the government is already offering you incentives to contribute to these types of programs – further offering tax deductibility of interest would be a tad too generous in their eyes. Which maybe it would be.

The Collateral and Loan Terms Do Not Determine Deductibility

Some Canadians assume that if their house is the bank's security for a loan, then the interest is not tax-deductible. This is important: the security offered for a loan has nothing to do with whether the interest expense is deductible. The main test is: *what did you do with the money that you borrowed?* And the investments you will purchase will be free-and-clear; they will not be collateral for the secured line of credit. This is because the mortgage lender has the house as collateral.

If you think about it, no bank is terribly concerned with what you are spending the borrowed money on once you draw it from the line of credit. They are unconcerned whether you are taking that borrowed cash and buying a car with it, going on vacation, throwing it on the campfire or investing.

Some people may assume that conventional loans with payments that include both an interest and a principal reduction component are, by their nature, in the non-deductible category. This is also not true. Again, the type of loan, whether interest-only or principal-plus-interest payments, whether secured by your home or not, does not impact whether the interest is deductible. What matters is, *to what purpose did you put the money that you borrowed?*

Consolidation of Bad Debt

Perhaps here is a good place to mention consolidation of non-deductible debt. Many of us – too many of us – carry a balance on our 10.99% or 19.99% credit card which we would like to pay off in its entirety each month but that seldom happens. Maybe you have a car loan with a rate that runs a little high? A personal line of credit at three points over prime, perhaps, that got used for the new roof? When you are applying for the new readvanceable mortgage with which you will implement *The Smith Manoeuvre*, you may have an opportunity to consolidate some or all of that expensive non-deductible consumer debt. If there is the space, you can pay out the 19.99% credit card debt or the personal line of credit balance with the new mortgage proceeds at a much lower rate.

The debt will still be non-deductible – we'll take care of that later via the conversion process – but for the time being it may quite likely be in your best interest to replace that $15,000 or so of 19.99% debt with 4.2% debt on the new mortgage. By doing so, instead of a mortgage of, say, $500,000, you would have a mortgage of $515,000 but your overall carrying costs of debt will decrease. At 19.99%, $15,000 worth of debt costs you $250 per month. At 4.2% it costs you $52.50 per month. That's almost $2,400 per year in savings, or 'salvaged payments', as we say. It is worth looking into with your *Smith Manoeuvre Certified Professional* advisor for certain.

Not Only Lower Your Payments but Increase Your Wealth

And here's the thing, by consolidating you can convert that debt into investments and tax deductions via the conversion process. Further, the salvaged payments can do even more for you. If you had been carrying that $250 monthly payment every month for who knows how long, then that means you have been able to 'afford' it (in a loose sense of the word). So after you refinance into the readvanceable mortgage and begin your *Smith Manoeuvre* journey, commit to continuing with that $250 per month outlay as a *mortgage prepayment.*

Two hundred fifty dollars going as a prepayment against your mortgage, generating you tax deductions and getting invested for your retirement each and every month versus $250 being simply the price to pay to continue to owe someone money for eternity? No-brainer. Remember the Cash Flow Diversion Accelerator? This is where it will apply – diverting salvaged consumer debt payments against the mortgage. It is hugely effective in converting your mortgage quicker, increasing the pace at which your tax deductions grow, and speeding up the accumulation of wealth in your *Personal Pension Plan*.

Preservation of Good Debt

So we've talked about consolidation of *bad* debt, but what about preservation of *good* debt? Some of you may have a personal line of credit which contains deductible debt already. Maybe you borrowed and then invested a few bucks – let's say $30,000 – into your own business, somebody else's business or mutual funds, and your accountant is deducting the interest costs. Fantastic! Again, whether you knew it at the time or not, you behaved as the wealthy do – you used borrowed money to invest.

Well, when you refinance into the readvanceable mortgage, you may have an opportunity to preserve the deductible debt if your borrowing power with the new mortgage allows. You may be currently paying a prime plus 3.5% rate on that deductible debt which does nice things for your tax refund, but if you have an opportunity to replace that with, let's say, a prime plus 0.5% rate on your new line of credit which comes with the readvanceable mortgage, you would choose to do so. Deductible or non-deductible, a lower rate means lower payments and more to invest directly and immediately for retirement.

So, on the line of credit portion, with the help of your *Smith Manoeuvre Certified Professional* investment advisor and/or mortgage broker, you would instruct any immediate borrowing power on that soon-to-be and forever-more deductible low-rate *secured* line of credit side (not the non-deductible loan portion side) to pay out the deductible debt currently residing on your personal *unsecured*, high-rate line of credit. If you were paying, let's say, $175 per month at 7% on that $30,000 of deductible debt when it was on your personal line of credit and now you're paying $100 per month at 4.5% on the secured line of credit, you are salvaging $75 per month in payments.

Same Payments, Only... Different

Well, if you could handle that payment before, you can handle it now – so start to prepay your new mortgage by the full $175 per month (again, Cash Flow Diversion Accelerator) and after the money runs through the mortgage and $100 is required to service the interest on the $30,000 secured deductible line of credit where it now resides, there is the difference of $75 per month that gets invested for your future. Each and every month. Prior to deductible debt preservation you were paying $175 per month in interest. Now you are paying $100 in interest and getting $75 invested and still generating tax deductions from that deductible balance you preserved.

The prepayment of the $175 per month will take lots of time off the amortization of that non-deductible mortgage debt, and you will be far better off even with just an extra $75 a month getting invested into the magic of compound growth.

The Smithman Calculator allows you to input amounts of non-deductible debt to be consolidated and deductible debt to be preserved and will show you the benefits of doing so. We also demonstrate this application in *The Smith Manoeuvre Homeowner Course* via more detailed process instruction and recorded step-by-step video instruction on *The Smithman Calculator* use.

Wealth Accumulation

In 1989, David Chilton wrote a very important book called *The Wealthy Barber*. You probably have heard of it and likely have read it yourself – if not, do yourself a favour and read it. It explains the value of consistency when it comes to a savings plan and advocates putting aside a percentage of your income for your future. The value of putting aside a percentage of your income, no matter what, on a consistent basis cannot be underestimated.

However, instead of just putting that money directly into an investment program, first use it to prepay that mortgage of yours to eliminate that non-deductible debt faster, then reborrow it to get invested to start generating tax deductions and start building your nest egg. It's the Chilton method to wealth creation used as a *Smith Manoeuvre* accelerator – Cash Flow Diversion, to be precise. David also published a follow-up called *The Wealthy Barber Returns*.

Saving versus Investing

Many Canadians own Canada Savings Bonds (CSBs), term deposits, or Guaranteed Investment Certificates (GICs). These are really *savings* systems as opposed to *investment* systems. There may well be times when something like a GIC is appropriate – short-term money holds, for example – but as an investment, they are not great. You are lending your hard-earned after-tax dollars to government or big businesses, such as the banks. In return, your dollars earn a very low rate of interest, and then at the end of the year, whatever small amount they did earn is taxed at your full tax rate – say 40%. So a bad 'investment' is made worse.

On the other hand, these savings vehicles are safe – even if the government is broke, they can always raise your taxes to get enough money from you in order to give you back the small percentage they need to give you as your interest, then at the end of the year they will tax you at 40% on what they gave you for interest, which they got from you in taxes at the beginning of this run-on sentence… The final humiliation is that your minuscule return on investment must then be depreciated by the inflation rate. This assumes you are interested in knowing the real rate of return. When you see it is negative or close to it, maybe your interest will turn to annoyance. Big tax on small interest is not good for your financial well-being.

So you are 'safe'… safely losing money, that is.

"How many millionaires do you know who have become wealthy by investing in savings accounts? I rest my case."
- Robert G. Allen

Three Months Income as an Emergency Fund

Many financial planners are still advising that you should have the equivalent of three to six months' income or expenses in cash in a CSB, term deposit, or savings account in case of an emergency. So now you've got $15,000 - $40,000 depreciating in value considering the rate of return (if there is one) isn't keeping up with inflation. Instead, what you may consider is procuring a personal line of credit which you reserve *only* for emergencies – you don't use it unless you need to. It costs nothing unless you do, and you have therefore just created the ability to use that $15,000 - $40,000 that is currently sitting in 'emergency cash' to instead prepay your mortgage and get it invested at a meaningful rate or return. Debt Swap it!

To reiterate, the Debt Swap is not only the process of liquidating existing paid-up investments for cash in order to prepay the mortgage and then reborrow to invest again – you can also Debt Swap with cash on hand.

So if you have three to six months of savings sitting somewhere in cash or near-cash, consider the Debt Swap after you procure a personal line of credit, if you have not already. If you invest in stocks, bonds, mutual funds, investment real estate, somebody else's business or your own business, your growth potential will increase significantly, and therefore your wealth, and the interest expense will be tax-deductible because you are borrowing with the expectation of earning income from your investments.

Some people will advise against having a line of credit waiting in the wings for emergencies because we humans are a weak lot. Pretty soon we end up classifying our desire for a little used convertible as an 'emergency' and off we go driving into the sunset in another depreciating (but fun) asset... Indeed, that may be the case for some people, but if you are a responsible person dedicated to your family's betterment and security, you can have the discipline to leave it alone. That's up to you.

Investing in Real Estate

You could buy investment real estate, but you will want to be well-versed in some of the considerations before jumping in. Many excellent business writers point to a few pressures on real estate as an investment class:

1. It is not a very liquid investment. If you want to sell it quickly, you may have difficulty.

2. One should not underestimate the amount of work that screening and dealing with renters entails.

3. It has been broadly forecast by demographers and financial experts such as Garth Turner that as the baby boomers continue to retire, some will downsize. In addition, the number of homebuyers coming on stream is a much smaller cohort than the cohort that is getting ready to retire. This double negative does not bode well for traditional single-family residential investment housing as the baby boomers continue to retire "en masse".

4. Your own home generally does better than revenue houses because your home is free of capital gains tax upon sale and revenue properties are not.

However, with all the above being said, there will certainly be areas and pockets out there which will be a good bet in this space if you are prepared to commit some time and effort into it; I just want to ensure anyone considering getting into investment real estate is doing their homework.

Alternatively, there are plenty of real estate investment trust (REITs) and real estate joint venture opportunities out there which enable you to buy diversified properties without being the one who has to fix the leaky pipes in winter after your tenant calls with a flooded bathroom. In fact, there are some quite creative investment opportunities out there relating to real estate. In *The Smith Manoeuvre Homeowner Course*, there is also an important discussion surrounding the financing and servicing goals of your investment property should you have one or be thinking about it.

What Else Is There?

Equities may be a good bet for the bulk of your investing, based on historic rates of return on investment. Equities have always done well if you stay invested and ignore the volatility. If you have no plans to sell your house, then it tends to matter little to you if house prices are dropping or rising – you don't pay much attention. We should learn to do the same with equity investments.

The scenario we paint for users of *The Smith Manoeuvre* is that when you invest in equities, you should be broadly diversified in different asset classes, you should lean to blue-chip and you should invest early, regularly and often. If you follow this advice you can avoid trying to time the market which is a losing proposition for investors. At least until you have the ability to predict the future. Volatility does not really hurt us if we are not trying to time the market and have a long time horizon of investment.

Now all the above being said, as I mention earlier, implementation of *The Smith Manoeuvre* requires only that you invest. What you invest in is entirely up to you. Just be sure to check with your advisor to ensure the investment you are considering qualifies for deductible interest on the borrowing.

What about RRSPs?

Some, but not all, financial advisors agree that an RRSP is a useful and profitable device for most Canadians. And there has been a long and continuous battle raging on the question "Is it better to use after-tax dollars to buy an RRSP or to make an extra payment on the mortgage?"

It's good that the amount you contribute to an RRSP is tax-deductible. It's bad that this deduction is a one-time event. It's good that the investments inside the RRSP can grow tax-free. It's bad that RRSP investments are taxed as 100% income when you de-register them. On and on it goes.

The naysayers point to the fact that more than one-third of eligible Canadians don't have an RRSP, and that most RRSPs are meagre in size. But maybe the reason so many have no RRSP or have small RRSPs has more to do with affordability than an aversion to RRSPs. Many people simply cannot afford them.

So, there is much discussion on whether or not to 'RRSP'. This animated discourse has been going on for years. Google "RRSP or mortgage" and you will find hundreds of articles arguing both sides of the issue (many compromise and solve the puzzle by suggesting you buy an RRSP instead of paying down your mortgage, then they suggest you apply your RRSP tax refund against your mortgage).

These hundreds of articles have been written without prior consideration of the natural positive effects we have seen that emanate from utilizing *The Smith Manoeuvre*. In many, but not all cases, it appears that a Canadian would choose to set up *The Smith Manoeuvre*, cash the RRSP, pay the tax, use the residue to make a lump sum reduction of the mortgage then immediately borrow back that money and invest it *outside* the RRSP. Again, here's the Debt Swap. If this is a profitable step, then it also likely follows that current monthly or regular cash flow that is contributing to RRSPs should cease. Instead it should be applied as monthly prepayments against the mortgage then reborrowed to invest in a non-registered account.

The mortgage would obviously be converted to deductible much quicker in this scenario. As soon as the conversion was accomplished so that all debt was now deductible, monthly RRSP purchases would resume.

Tax-Free Savings Accounts (TFSA)

Starting in 2009, the federal government of Canada proclaimed that qualifying Canadians could enjoy tax-free growth and tax-free withdrawals from a new Tax-Free Savings Account program. The maximum allowable annual contributions have fluctuated over the years and these accounts operate differently than RRSPs, but the principle of the scheme is the same – incentivize Canadians to save for their future in order to provide better financial prospects for individual Canadians and Canada in general.

As for the differences between a TFSA and an RRSP, a TFSA does not offer the contributor any tax deductions for the year of contribution but there is no tax upon withdrawal; as for an RRSP, there are tax deductions for the year of contribution but withdrawals are fully taxed.

There are other differences but they are not really for discussion here – more detailed discussion is offered in *The Smith Manoeuvre Homeowner Course*. The point is that, just like RRSP contributions, dependent on your personal condition, a good advisor will be able to show you the financial advantages of using any available cash (if there is any) to prepay the mortgage and then invest outside of a registered program as opposed to forgoing the mortgage conversion process.

It Can Be Quantified

There are so many variables involved when dealing with RRSPs and TFSAs and mortgages simultaneously that it is impossible to make blanket recommendations. Accordingly, we suggest that first you get your *Smith Manoeuvre* up and running. Then you and your accredited *Smith Manoeuvre Certified Professional* advisor can take the time to analyze your specific circumstances to determine whether you are financially better off to sell or hold your RRSP/TFSA during your mortgage conversion period, and/or continue with registered contributions or discontinue and apply funds to the mortgage conversion process.

The comparison of before-tax and after-tax incomes is an important way to correctly analyze the impact of financial decisions we need to make in life.

Summary on Investment

Specific types of investments, including tax treatment and examples of what qualifies for deductible interest and what doesn't, is offered in *The Smith Manoeuvre Homeowner Course*, but know that *The Smith Manoeuvre* does not require that you choose one asset class over another. The strategy provides investment cash flow starting immediately. You will choose which assets you want to gather at which time and in which order. We encourage diversification, but that is your decision to make. We encourage blue-chip, but maybe your pleasure quotient arising from risk-taking is more important to you than surety of capital.

You may be starting to feel comfortable that *The Smith Manoeuvre* seems logical and reasonable in its claims, so corroborate your intuition by comparing mathematical comparisons of *Your* Way versus *The Smith Manoeuvre* Way. To see how much your financial future can be improved, all you need to do is input your personal assumptions and mortgage facts into *The Smithman Calculator*. The improvement in wealth accumulation that is engineered by *The Smith Manoeuvre* will surprise you and these excellent improvements require no new cash flow from you.

Your gains do not require you to increase your debt either. Debt levels do not have to get any higher than where they are when you start the program.

The Smith Manoeuvre is totally self-funding. Even the cost of the deductible interest expense on your new investment line of credit is allowed for. The software is very powerful and is designed to calculate and reserve the amount of interest needed to service the investment line on an ongoing basis. This expense is accommodated out of the increasing amount of principal reduction that occurs when a mortgage payment is paid. The difference is the actual amount that is available to be invested each month. More on this little 'magic trick' in the next section.

> "Try to save something while your salary is small; it's impossible to save after you begin to earn more."
> **- Jack Benny**

CHAPTER 7

COMMON MYTHS, MISTAKES AND OTHER THINGS TO KNOW

There is a lot of misinformation out there folks, so beware. Just recently I came across a piece on the internet written by a financial journalist for publication by one of our very well-known broadcasters. This journalist explained *The Smith Manoeuvre* was accomplished by 'selling all non-registered portfolio holdings and using them as a down payment on the mortgage after which you could reborrow to invest'.

Firstly, what this appears to describe is the Debt Swap, which you hopefully will recognize by now. The Debt Swap is simply an accelerator, it is not *The Smith Manoeuvre* itself. Secondly, by implementing the Debt Swap, you are not using the funds as a 'down payment'. If that were the case, you would not be able to reborrow and invest as it states above considering the mortgage lender requires the 'down payment' to remain as equity in the house. What the author should have done is simply replaced 'down payment' with 'prepayment' and noted that what was being described was simply an accelerator for *The Smith Manoeuvre.*

Misinformation, Misunderstanding and Myths Abound!

This demonstrates two problems out there in the ether. One – many people, including very educated financial professionals, believe that the Debt Swap equals *The Smith Manoeuvre*, and therefore, that *The Smith Manoeuvre* equals the Debt Swap. Secondly, just because someone is in a position of 'authority' doesn't mean we can assume they are fully knowledgeable of which they speak.

We are training real estate agents, mortgage brokers, investment advisors, conveyancing lawyers/notaries, insurance agents and accountants across the country as accredited *Smith Manoeuvre Certified Professionals* so you can enlist the services of someone you can trust to have taken the extensive course and examination. In addition, you can also go to www.smithman.net to take *The Smith Manoeuvre Homeowner Course* (don't worry - no test!) to ensure you are fully clear on the strategy so that, among other things, you can recognize when someone you are relying on to help you doesn't have it right. It could be costly otherwise.

Myth – The Growth Rate Must at Least Equal the Interest Rate

Another thing we see quite frequently are people explaining that in order for *The Smith Manoeuvre* to be worthwhile, you need to earn at least the same rate of growth on your investments as the rate on the line of credit from which you are borrowing each month. In other words, if my line of credit rate is 4.0%, then the return on my investments must be 4.0% at the very minimum in order for it to start to make sense.

We must consider that if you have borrowed to invest in a qualified investment whereby you can deduct the interest, you can deduct *100%* of the interest, which in itself is great. However, owning investments that are largely going to render you dividends or capital gains means that the return on the investments *will not be* 100% taxable. Also great. Further, with capital gains, only half of the gain is taxed and only upon sale of the asset, so this taxation is deferred – great again! Effectively, the growth is compounding tax-deferred. A big plus. Taxation later is much better than taxation now considering the effect of inflation.

Just remember that as a reasonable investor, I can fully *expect* the returns on my investment portfolio to be less than 4.0% every once in a while. But I can also expect that my portfolio will perform significantly better than 4.0% every once in a while. So while the line of credit rate from the lender may be consistent, my portfolio returns may fluctuate widely – sometimes even into the negative. But what is so beautiful about this strategy is that with such a long time horizon – ideally for as long as you live – the market risk curve gets very flat indeed. It is not uncommon to see 6%, 8%, 10% average returns for common investments.

Nominal Rate of Interest vs Real Rate of Interest

To bring in another aspect of rates of interest versus portfolio growth is the fact that the rate you see on your line of credit statement isn't what you are actually paying when everything is factored in. Related to the point above, let's say that your portfolio growth was, in fact, the same as the line of credit interest rate you see on your monthly mortgage statement – 4.0% growth and 4.0% interest rate. We need to take into consideration the fact that the nominal rate of interest you are paying on that line of credit is not the actual, or real, rate. Because the interest is tax-deductible, the real rate – what you are actually paying, deductions considered – is lower than the nominal rate – the rate you see printed on the statement.

Let's take someone at a marginal tax rate of 30%. This person, with her $100,000 line of credit balance at 4.0% pays $333 in interest for the month. But due to the fact that the interest is tax-deductible, she is able to take that $333 for the month off her taxable income which leads to a tax refund. Money back in her pocket from the government. So, if she is at the 30% marginal tax rate then the actual rate she is paying on that borrowed money is only 2.80%.

Myth – The Investment Portfolio Needs to Earn More Than the Line of Credit Rate in Order to Service the LOC

Tied further to the above points is the common misunderstanding that if your investments are not earning more than the rate on your line of credit, then you aren't able to service the increasing interest costs on that line of credit considering the balance keeps increasing each month as fast as the non-deductible principal balance of the loan portion is going down.

As we keep on telling you that no new money is required from your pockets for the process, it is understandable that the immediate thought would be that your investments need to be generating increasing monthly cash flow to service the increasing monthly (deductible) interest expense on the line of credit. But we need to consider the increasing efficiency of the mortgage payment.

Every mortgage payment I make is the same. Each month it is a constant amount, let's say $3,000. The very first month, $1,800 of that payment goes to non-deductible interest and $1,200 goes to reduce principal. As you will be very clear by this point, I will be able to reborrow that $1,200 and get it invested. Great. All is well. Considering it is the first month of the process, there was no previous balance on the line of credit and therefore no interest payment to make that month. The full $1,200 that was made available to reborrow got invested.

The second month, however, due to the amortizing nature of the mortgage loan, out of that same $3,000 mortgage payment, a little bit less goes to interest. Why? Because for the past 30 days my mortgage rate has been applied to a lower balance than the first month considering I had reduced that balance by $1,200. Let's say only $1,795 goes to interest. Well, if $1,795 went to interest, that means $1,205 went to reduce the principal balance. And after I reborrow that $1,205 and get $1,200 invested, there is still five dollars in my *Smith Manoeuvre Chequing Account*. Perfect. My mortgage lender comes into that account as instructed and takes that five dollars as interest on the first month's borrowing of $1,200.

The third month, $1,790 goes to interest and $1,210 goes against principal and is available to reborrow into my *Smith Manoeuvre Chequing Account*. Again, my constant monthly reinvestment amount of $1,200 is taken by the investment company I have chosen, thereby leaving $10 in the bank account. That's good because this third month the interest expense on the line of credit is pretty close to $10 considering there is a month's interest on *two* months' balance.

The above discussion explains how *The Smith Manoeuvre* is fully self-funding, and the concept that allows this is referred to as the 'increasing efficiency of the mortgage payment'. More details on this are found in *The Smith Manoeuvre Homeowner Course*.

Leverage...or Is It?

One of the discussions we experience with others regarding the strategy is that around 'leverage'. Leverage being defined as 'borrowing to invest', in this case. We contend that

The Smith Manoeuvre is not a leveraging strategy, it is a *debt conversion* strategy. There is a difference. Canadians who implement *The Smith Manoeuvre* do so because they already have the debt. They have a mortgage already. Or if they don't quite yet have a mortgage, they will soon, whether they implement *The Smith Manoeuvre* or not. But prior to implementation of the strategy, the leverage has already occurred – it occurred when the bank loaned you that $300-, $500-, $700,000 to buy your house.

With *The Smith Manoeuvre*, you are not acquiring any new debt, you are simply changing the nature of the existing debt from bad debt to good debt, and in the process getting to enjoy a number of very pleasant things like tax deductions, the hastened elimination of expensive non-deductible mortgage payments and the accrual of investment assets to help finance your retirement.

Yes, I will agree that looked at strictly in isolation – that one step out of a few whereby I borrow from the line of credit – leverage has taken place. But that is not the whole story and we simply cannot look at this one event without taking into considering the whole process, which we do in depth in *The Smith Manoeuvre Homeowner Course.*

That being said, investing with borrowed money will magnify losses and gains. Also, the fact that you are using someone else's money for your potential gain must come with the recognition that they may eventually, unsurprisingly, want their money back regardless where the value of your investments sits. The Ontario Securities Commission website has a section which further discusses borrowing to invest and lists some questions to ask yourself.

Further, there are good books out there on the subject of borrowing to invest which go into further depth about things to know. On our website we have a list of suggested readings on a number of personal finance-related topics.

Common Mistakes

The Smith Manoeuvre is not a complicated strategy by concept. If we boil it down, we find that all we are doing is accessing monthly mortgage principal reductions so we have funds to invest, and where possible, applying the accelerators. And because we are borrowing to invest, we are generating tax deductions leading to tax refunds which we are then able to apply as a mortgage prepayment once a year and subsequently get that amount invested as well.

All this leads to a great reduction in the time it takes to eliminate that expensive non-deductible mortgage debt and a very tidy accrual of investment assets that otherwise would simply not exist. So there it is in a nutshell. However, when it comes down to the actual implementation, just like anything else in life, if done wrong, there are consequences. So let's go through a number of common mistakes in this section to ensure smooth sailing...

HELOC vs Readvanceable – Same Thing, Right?

When you look to refinance with the goal of implementing *The Smith Manoeuvre*, be careful if someone says what you want is a HELOC. This stands for Home Equity Line of Credit. It is similar to the line of credit facility you will find with a readvanceable mortgage, but a straight HELOC is not what you want.

Very generally, a HELOC is a lending component from the bank that takes into account the total available loan limit based on the value of your house, less any outstanding mortgage balance. So effectively, if the total loan limit for your circumstance is $400,000 but you only have $300,000 currently owing against the house, a HELOC will be extended for $100,000.

However, while the HELOC will allow you to take out that $100,000 right away to invest if you wish (Prime the Pump), once you withdraw it, the available credit is gone, not to return unless you go back in to the lawyer or notary's office to refinance it and pay the requisite fees, not to mention the hassle of requalifying. It does not readvance. It does not increase its lending limit dollar-for-dollar in real-time as the non-deductible loan portion further decreases with your regular monthly mortgage payment and any prepayments. It's a one-shot deal. No good.

That being said, terminology is going to vary between person and industry, so at the very least, if someone insists on calling it a HELOC, make sure that it is a HELOC connected to the amortizing loan portion and will *readvance* automatically in real time.

All This Available Credit!

When you refinance into a readvanceable mortgage you may have an immediate available balance on the line of credit side of the mortgage because the value of the house went up since you last financed, or your credit score/income circumstance has improved since last time and the bank is willing to lend you just a bit more money. And you may choose not to 'Prime the Pump' but instead let that excess equity stay available to you on an ongoing basis, which is fine.

But what is not fine is forgetting down the road what that line of credit is there for.

Many times have I seen people all of a sudden realize that they have available credit – maybe they had forgotten it was there? – and use it to replace a busted hot water boiler or repave their driveway. No, the secured line of credit is *no-touchy* unless your advisor says it's okay. You want to be sure that any available credit is used only for deductible purposes.

Put the Money to Work, Don't Let It Just Sit There

Another common lapse is trusting yourself to get it invested on a monthly basis and not setting the monthly investment contribution from the *Smith Manoeuvre Chequing Account* to occur automatically. If your monthly investment program is not automatic, there will likely be times where you forget to get the monthly amount invested – maybe you go on vacation – and there will be a buildup of funds in the *Smith Manoeuvre Chequing Account*. Or even if you have set up a monthly investment contribution to occur, the amount for which it is set is too low and there is a buildup in the *Smith Manoeuvre Chequing Account* over time of funds not getting invested. And if these funds are not getting invested, they are not working for you and you are simply paying interest on borrowed money that isn't growing. This can also open you up to a CRA challenge as the money has been borrowed but not invested.

Frequently check the month-end balance of that *Smith Manoeuvre Chequing Account* to ensure you don't let it build up to over maybe one- or two-month's buffer, whatever you're comfortable with.

Ahh, Christmas Debt…

It never fails. At least once a year we open the statement and see what we were expecting to see but didn't want to see nonetheless. We have a bigger-than-usual credit card balance and we would like to be rid of it sooner rather than later, so we look around to see where we can find funds to pay it off, or at least down as much as possible. Whatever you do, do not check your *Smith Manoeuvre Chequing Account* balance and get the idea that it can solve your problems.

Firstly, at the end of any given month, there should be as close to zero a balance in that *Smith Manoeuvre Chequing Account* as possible and therefore should hold little temptation, but if there is a balance in there, do not use it for credit card payments.

If you use funds in the *Smith Manoeuvre Chequing Account* to pay a credit card bill or service a personal line of credit that holds non-deductible debt, you are polluting the purity of the secured line of credit of your *Smith Manoeuvre* mortgage.

The money may be just sitting in that account but the point here is not what it's doing at that moment, it's where it came from. And if you are following the program as you should be, the only way that money got into that *Smith Manoeuvre Chequing Account* in the first place is because you instructed a withdrawal from the secured line of credit. Therefore it is borrowed money that is destined to either service the deductible interest of the line of credit or get invested. If you pay your Christmas Visa with that money, you have borrowed to consume and you have just mixed new non-deductible debt with deductible *Smith Manoeuvre* line of credit debt and your accountant will almost certainly take you off their Christmas card list.

And the same goes for prepaying the mortgage. Sometimes people may see an excess in the *Smith Manoeuvre Chequing Account* and think they can use it to prepay their non-deductible mortgage, but again, that would be using borrowed money from the line of credit for consumption when we want to keep it purely deductible.

That money in that *Smith Manoeuvre Chequing Account* is only there because you have implemented *The Smith Manoeuvre* – otherwise you wouldn't see it – so pretend it isn't there when life, which would get in your way regardless, starts to get in your way.

Unexpected Expenses

It is to be expected that we will run into financial issues in the course of our lives whereby $5,000, $10,000 or more would alleviate a particularly cash-strapped time. Maybe the roof all of a sudden needs to be repaired or the car finally gave up the ghost. It can be tempting to look at the large investment portfolio you have built up via *The Smith Manoeuvre* and think about selling $20,000 of investment assets in order to buy a new car, but a number of complicating things happen when you do that.

Firstly, you will get taxed if you have made any gains on the investment. Capital gains tax is the best type of tax out there because it is your tax rate applied to only half the gain, not the full gain, but it is tax nonetheless. Secondly, by redeeming that $20,000 you are foregoing future growth on that investment. If you redeem $20,000 of investments that were earning 8%, then you are missing out on $29,797 over the course of five years; $98,536 over the course of 20 years. So it adds up. And if we look at that $98,536 in 20 years, the monthly cash flow that it could generate at that time, when cash flow is very, very important to you, could be significant.

One of the biggest reasons that you may not want to liquidate those assets is because it may pollute the deductibility of the line of credit. The reason is this: originally the investments that you are now selling were purchased with borrowed money from the line of credit. By turning around and selling the asset and using the redemption proceeds for anything other than investing into a different type of security or making a payment against that deductible line of credit from whence it came, you may be changing the nature of the original borrowing from deductible to non-deductible. Your *Smith Manoeuvre Certified Professional* accountant can help with this determination. I would advise that you consider how you would have taken care of this unexpected expense if you did not have the investments at your disposal, if you had never implemented *The Smith Manoeuvre* which generated these assets for you in the first place, if you will. Again, try to pretend these assets don't exist, at least until you hit retirement.

If There Is No Other Way...

If, however, this is the only way to fund that new car or roof and there are no other cash or borrowing options considering your father-in-law doesn't like you, then in order to isolate the newly non-deductible borrowing related to the redemption you could consider conducting a balance transfer – basically shifting a corresponding amount of debt from the line of credit over to the non-deductible amortizing loan portion. This balance transfer process is quite commonly utilized but it must be done correctly. I elaborate on this in *The Smith Manoeuvre Homeowner Course.*

Open Account, Not Registered

Sometimes people will decide they want to generate additional tax benefits by contributing the investment assets they have accrued in their non-registered *Smith Manoeuvre* investment portfolio to a tax-sheltered investment such as an RRSP.

While investment assets in open accounts (non-registered) can be contributed in-kind in a technical sense, there may be tax consequences, for one thing, but for another, by doing so you may be changing the nature of the original borrowing from the line of credit from deductible to non-deductible considering that the Canada Revenue Agency will not allow you to deduct interest on money borrowed to contribute to a tax-sheltered investment such as an RRSP or TFSA.

So, if anyone recommends you do this make sure they understand clearly that the investments were originally purchased with borrowed money – there is further explanation in *The Smith Manoeuvre Homeowner Course* as to why this would not be an advised move.

These Mistakes Can Be Avoided

With *The Smith Manoeuvre* we are dealing with investing, accounting and the Canada Revenue Agency. These factors make it very important that all aspects of the strategy are set up and implemented appropriately and rules followed. It also requires long-term discipline and stick-to-itiveness.

For these reasons it is highly recommended that you ensure any financial professionals you enlist to help you with your journey – realtors, mortgage brokers, investment advisors, real estate lawyers/notaries, insurance agents and accountants – are *Smith Manoeuvre Certified Professional* accredited. You can direct your preferred professional to the accreditation program at www.smithman.net if he or she is not accredited already.

Other Things to Know

Here I will touch on some other things to be aware of and answer some questions you may have. There is an FAQ section on the www.smithman.net website but here are some other things to be aware of.

What if You Move?

A concern from some readers might revolve around the intent to change homes in the future. Do not let that prospect dissuade you from implementing *The Smith Manoeuvre* now, even if you know you may be moving. It is not a complicated matter to engineer the sale/purchase so that your deductible loan stays deductible even after you move. Essentially, the new readvanceable mortgage proceeds attached to the house you are buying will be used to pay out the existing deductible debt attached to the house you are selling. That way some or all of the original deductible debt can be preserved and the original use of the funds borrowed to invest can be traced from the old house to the new house.

There are processes to follow for this procedure but your planner and your broker will work together to keep you enjoying the benefits of *The Smith Manoeuvre* whether you had already completed the conversion on the original house or are still in the process of doing so when you move. This is further discussed in detail in *The Smith Manoeuvre Homeowner Course.*

What Does This Cost Me to Implement?

When initially refinancing from a mortgage that will not enable you to implement *The Smith Manoeuvre* into a readvanceable mortgage that will, there will be costs associated such as appraisal cost, legal/notary fees, title search/insurance, prepayment penalty, etc., but in many cases it may be possible to have some expenses covered by the institutions and organizations with whom you are dealing, or they can be wrapped into the new mortgage balance so nothing or next to nothing needs to come from your pocket to complete the refinance.

Except for any modest expenses associated with setting up financing, this strategy requires no ongoing cash from your resources. *The Smith Manoeuvre* is completely self-funding. In fact, to the contrary, this may be the first financial strategy you have seen where your family actually will begin receiving an annual cash flow that is free and tax-free at the same time. This is new money to your family courtesy of the tax department who will be sending you tax refund cheques because your interest expense will start giving you tax deductions to claim.

The 65% Loan-To-Value Rule

Back in September 2012, the Office of the Superintendent of Financial Institutions (OSFI) implemented the 65% HELOC rule. Essentially, for reasons explained as promoting prudent residential mortgage underwriting procedures, federally regulated financial institutions (e.g. banks) were required to lend not over 65% loan-to-value (LTV) on interest-only lines of credit. The total loan from the mortgage lender to the homeowner could go higher – indeed, a readvanceable mortgage will lend up to 80% LTV on a principal-plus-interest loan – but for any interest-only component, 65% became the upper limit.

So in other words, if a homeowner looking for a readvanceable mortgage had more than 35% equity in the house, no problem – they can borrow up to 65% of the value of the house in the form of a non-deductible principal-plus-interest amortizing loan and structure it to set to work converting that non-deductible debt to deductible right away and continuously, smooth as a billiard ball.

That being said, if the homeowner required the full 80% then different approaches may need to be taken depending on their specific type of readvanceable mortgage. In *The Smith Manoeuvre Homeowner Course* I discuss some of the various readvanceable mortgages currently available; some of which allow immediate readvancing, even at up to 80% loan-to-value, and some which don't.

A Quick Word on Rental Properties

Frequently people will ask whether they can execute *The Smith Manoeuvre* on a rental property. Recall that *The Smith Manoeuvre* is a *debt conversion strategy*. We are converting onerous non-deductible debt to beneficial deductible debt. That is the objective of the strategy, with the benefits being getting rid of that non-deductible debt in record time and simultaneously building up an investment portfolio so you have a significantly better chance at enjoying your golden years in comfort.

Considering that a rental property is a business, any borrowing to acquire or invest in that business is tax-deductible to begin with, namely the mortgage you took on to buy the investment property. So there is no need to convert non-deductible debt as there is none in the first place. While a rental property, as a proprietorship, does not present an opportunity to convert bad debt to good in and of itself, it certainly presents a great opportunity to assist in the conversion of your own non-deductible principal residence mortgage, as we have seen earlier as per the Cash Flow Dam Accelerator.

There is also an important consideration as to whether you wish to make interest-only payments on your rental property mortgage or principal-plus-interest payments to reduce the balance over time. This depends on your goals and has important implications on the value of your personal investment portfolio over time – more on this in *The Smith Manoeuvre Homeowner Course.*

Deductible Uses of Borrowed Funds

At this point it would be a good idea to explain why the interest on the line of credit is fully deductible. After all, you will recognize that on a monthly basis two things are happening out of that *Smith Manoeuvre Chequing Account* – the funds that get pulled from the line of credit into that *Smith Manoeuvre Chequing Account* are going to a) investment, and b) to interest payments on the line of credit. We have talked at length about the fact that if you borrow to invest you can deduct the interest from your income but what if you are borrowing to pay interest itself? The Canada Revenue Agency (CRA) specifically advises in Section 20(1)(c) of the Tax Act that if interest on a loan is deductible, then so is the interest on the interest. In other words, if I borrow to pay interest on a loan that is deductible, the interest on that interest is also deductible. Beautiful.

Market Risk

With *The Smith Manoeuvre*, in order to speed up the elimination of your expensive, non-deductible mortgage, you must invest. And if you are getting invested, you are subjecting yourself to market risk. The markets and your investments will increase in value and decrease in value. That is for certain.

However, 'what' you invest in is very important. There are risky investments out there and not-so-risky investments. Even not-so-risky investments will fluctuate in value. That being said, if you are putting your dollars into investments with little risk, you are able to minimize the market risk. And you can and should diversify your investment portfolio so that when one asset class lags, another that you own can pick up the slack. Further, *The Smith Manoeuvre* is not a short-term, mid-term, or even long-term investment strategy. It is *very* long term – as long as you can get. And the longer you are invested in quality securities, the less market volatility affects you. In fact, by remaining invested ultra-long term, market volatility is greatly levelled out. The very long-term nature of *The Smith Manoeuvre* significantly flattens the risk curve.

Consider this – if you take $10,000 and put it under the mattress for 25 years, it will be *valued* at precisely $10,000 when you pull it out. But will it be *worth* $10,000? No. While that $10,000 may buy you a *good* motorcycle today, in 25 years it may only buy you a *good* bicycle. If you do not participate in the economy and invest you will lose. You will lose to inflation. And even if you save with GICs and only manage to keep up to inflation, don't you have bigger aspirations than putting money away that could buy you a good motorcycle now only to be able to buy an equivalently good motorcycle in 25 years?

No, we want to see our money grow, to increase our net worth. And the only way to do that is to invest. This is what the wealthy do, and haven't you already promised yourself that you are going to start to act like the wealthy? Consult a good, trustworthy, accredited *Smith Manoeuvre Certified Professional* investment advisor and let him or her help you commit to the long term and invest wisely to minimize risk.

Interest Rates

As you will be maintaining your debt levels, you will be subject to rate risk. That being said, you already have a mortgage so you already are exposed to rate risk. Sure, you may have locked in your rate for the next five years but do you know where rates will be when it comes time to renew your mortgage? If you do, please let me know…we have lots to talk about! That being said, if you were actually paying down your mortgage over time, generally your rate risk would go down as well considering that all things being equal, you are paying interest on an increasingly smaller balance.

But by keeping your debt constant, you will maintain rate risk going forward. I do not wish to diminish 'rate risk' but as we have seen, the increasing efficiency of the regular mortgage payment services the interest expense on the investment loan so it does not have to come out of your pocket. And with the help of *The Smithman Calculator*, we can see that interest rates have to be pretty darn high before the net benefit of the strategy is reduced to simply break even.

So you will be paying interest on the money that you have borrowed and, for certain, rates will go up and rates will go down. Sometimes you will be paying more and sometimes you will be paying less. But this is expected – we know that this is the case. And the long-term nature of this strategy greatly flattens out the rate risk curve as well.

In *The Smith Manoeuvre Homeowner Course* we look in detail at how varying interest rates on the secured line of credit portion of your readvanceable mortgage affect your numbers in the video demonstration of *The Smithman Calculator* tutorial.

Rules Can Change

The CRA and the Ministry of Finance raised a trial balloon in 2004 regarding the possibility of changing the tax rules regarding interest deductibility. The suggestions generated mountains of responses from professionals across the country with comments ranging from "draconian" to "hare-brained".

If these changes were to be made as proposed, you will be affected as far as your deductions are concerned. But even if the worst happened, and it could, you will still operate *The Smith Manoeuvre*. Note the 'net improvement in family net worth' value of $292,822 at the bottom of figure 7.1. This is the net benefit to a family with a mortgage of $400,000 at 4.5%, but the calculator has been instructed to *not* apply tax refunds against the mortgage as annual prepayments.

Fig. 7.1

However, when you look at figure 7.2 where the calculator *has* been instructed to apply refunds against the mortgage, you will see the return increases by just over $138,000 to $431,038.

Fig. 7.2

In other words, around two-thirds of the effect of *The Smith Manoeuvre* comes from benefits of owning your investments *now* instead of *later*. About one-third of the benefit is the effect of converting to tax-deductible interest.

We will be supremely disappointed in the government if we lose the important benefit of tax-deductible interest when we invest and we will vote out the government silly enough to make such an abysmal decision, but we will still continue to operate *The Smith Manoeuvre*. In any event, your *Smith Manoeuvre Certified Professionals* will be kept up to date by us with any changes as regards regulations and rules so that you will be able to continue to operate your *Smith Manoeuvre* as effectively as possible.

Try to Keep Emotion out of It

Money is an emotional subject, no question. We work hard for it and we want to make sure we protect it. And when we are investing, we naturally can get emotional. And that is fine, but the problem arises when we let emotion or fear or greed overcome sensibility and discipline. I am not creating some breakthrough theory when I say one of the most common – and painful – investing mistakes is buying high and selling low.

When markets are really rolling hot, we as individuals get all excited and caught up in the hype and scrape together what dollars we can to get invested. Right at the top of the market. Then the markets go down – as I promise you they do – and we get caught up in the fear. The world is ending and if we don't flush our investments now, we are going to lose everything! So we sell at a loss. Six months, eight months later – well after the markets have already turned north again – the hype returns, and we feel we are going to miss out big time if we don't get back into the markets. At the top. Again. Then the markets go south and we repeat the loss.

> "Buy when everyone else is selling and hold until everyone else is buying. That's not just a catchy slogan. It's the very essence of successful investing."
> **- J. Paul Getty**

A Bit Deeper Look Into This…

Our amateur do-it-yourself investor, Adam, bought Royal Bank stock just before the peak of the market cycle. He's glad he did because he watched his shares go from $90 to $95. Not bad. But then the markets turn and he gets a little concerned. Back down to $90, then to $85 a share. Nervous. Down to $82. Scared. Down to $80. That's it! With all the bad news out there and the professionals prognosticating about further declines, the falling sky and the cracks in the earth, he decides to sell. Adam looks around for someone onto whom he can unload his RBC shares:

Professional Trader (PT):	"Hi Adam, word on the street is that you are looking to shed your RBC shares."
Adam:	"Yeah, yeah, yeah! What will you give me for them?"
PT:	"How about $79 a share?"
Adam:	"Done! Sold! Thank you so much, PT!"
PT:	"You're welcome." *Be seeing you soon, Adam…*

So Adam is pleased with himself that although he took a haircut and lost a significant amount of money, he is at least out before the world ended. Adam has his first decent night of sleep in weeks. He still keeps an eye on the markets though and notices that they appear to be holding level. "Yeah, right! This ain't the end of this slump…" But the markets don't turn south again. They hold and shift up. Slowly and tentatively at first. But then momentum gains and there's a lot of increases and fast.

However, feeling a bit burned from the first experience, Adam still sits on the sidelines considering this is likely just a short-term pop. RBC shares hit $90, then $95, then $100 and $110. At this point Adam is noting that everything seems to be doing well and he's listening to the TV shows and reading the financial papers and everyone seems to be quite confident about where things are headed. So, feeling that he can't afford to miss out on all this upside, he goes looking for some RBC shares…

Here We Go Again

Adam:	"Hey PT! How you doing? Long time no see! Listen, I need to get back in. You still have those RBC shares I sold you?"
PT:	"Well, yes, I do. You want some?"

Adam:	"Absolutely! Things are looking great, eh?"
PT:	"Yeah - real hot market! $111 per share."
Adam:	"Done and done! Thanks PT!"
PT:	"You're welcome." *Be seeing you soon, Adam...*

I won't explain what happens next to our dear Adam because I'm quite certain you know it's rinse and repeat. While Adam is repeatedly buying high and selling low, our professional trader is buying low and selling high.

And so it goes for so many inexperienced investors. Caught up in the excitement when markets are hot, they buy in; scared and timid when markets go down and they fire off their holdings. Think about it – isn't it interesting that the stock market is the only market in the world where when things go on sale people run for the exits...

The thing about *The Smith Manoeuvre* strategy is that if you diligently execute it as designed, you need not worry about market timing or squaring off with the professional traders because if you are enlisting the services of a *Smith Manoeuvre Certified Professional* investment advisor you have professional traders on your side and are taking a large part of emotional risk out of the equation. So, schedule the purchase of investments to occur automatically on a monthly basis, let the professionals managing your investments decide when to buy and when to sell, and try to keep your cool.

I promise you markets will go up and markets will go down, and sometimes it may make us a bit nervous, but if we look at stock market indices like the TSX, S&P or Dow, we will notice that not once in history have they failed to proceed higher after a market correction compared to the previous high just before the correction. Not once.

"The Stock Market is designed to transfer money from the Active to the Patient."
- Warren Buffett

Complacency

Perhaps the biggest risk is doing nothing at all. We know for certain that if we do not participate in the economy, if we do not put our dollars to work for us via putting it to work for others, we will earn 0% return. Actually, we will earn a negative return considering inflation – if we are earning 0% but the value of money is declining over time, then we are really looking at a negative return. Negatives can be good – medical tests, for example, or on Star Trek: "Spock, are we on a trajectory to be sucked into that black hole?", "Negative, Captain"… but when we are talking about the value of our money, negatives are most definitely *not* good.

Complacency encompasses not only making a conscious decision *not* to invest, but also *not* bothering to learn about how we can improve our wealth or, at the very least, protect ourselves. I will admit that, for many, the subject of personal finance can be a little dry – as proof, I offer this book as evidence… We are increasingly exposed to myriad entertainment options, we have busy lives, we like to enjoy ourselves and our friends and family. It can be difficult to find the discipline to sit down and read a book or attend a personal finance seminar. But it is so terribly important. We need to educate ourselves in order to be able to provide ourselves and loved ones with the best chance of financial security.

And part of this is ensuring the youth of today are properly prepared for their future. It is important to educate your children on personal finances as well. The education system is not doing it, so who is? Kids should be exposed to education surrounding money as early on as possible and from professionals. Get them reading! Bring them to a personal finance seminar or watch a webinar with them!

Educate yourself and those close to you as much as possible and take action. Do something.

"Procrastination is the enemy of your financial success."
- Fraser Smith

You May Be Ready for *The Smith Manoeuvre,* You May Not

There are rules and regulations in the mortgage industry that will dictate whether you are able to implement *The Smith Manoeuvre* as regards acquiring the appropriate financing. If you're not ready yet, get ready. Do what you need to in order to get your consumer debt levels, credit score or high-ratio mortgage to the point that you can qualify for a readvanceable mortgage.

Also, depending on your personal condition, *The Smith Manoeuvre* may not be appropriate for you from an investment point of view. It is the case that investment advisors and financial planners need to adhere to the guidelines of their applicable industry regulators, and this may restrict a homeowner if they wish to enlist the services of a regulated financial professional. Also, depending on your risk tolerance or age, it may not be appropriate from a regulatory standpoint. Talk to your accredited *Smith Manoeuvre Certified Professional* investment advisor – have a discussion – and he or she will be able to offer guidance.

The Smith Manoeuvre Decelerator – '*The Smith Manoeuvre Lite*'

With all this talk of accelerators, it is certainly a bit odd to mention a 'decelerator', but indeed, for those so inclined, there is a way to *slow* the mortgage conversion process of *The Smith Manoeuvre*. I mention this method here (and elaborate in *The Smith Manoeuvre Homeowner Course*) because I didn't want every reader to think that this was an 'all-or-nothing' type of financial strategy. This would likely have pushed some readers away from implementing the strategy and that would be too bad because even if some don't feel they are ready to go whole hog with the 'maintain your total debt' premise of this book, there are ways that you can still improve your financial condition by taking it slower.

Not all people are 'in for a penny, in for a pound' people, and the last thing I would want to see are people turning away because they didn't know they could take a bit of a slower approach to financial freedom, at least to start, and then ramp it up later – or even reverse it – if they so choose to do so.

Insurance

Considering you are restructuring your finances in preparation of implementing *The Smith Manoeuvre* and will be sitting down with your *Smith Manoeuvre Certified Professional* advisors in any event, it will be a good time to review your insurance situation as well – life insurance, mortgage insurance, disability and critical illness insurance…insurance of all fun and rosy sorts.

We suggest that you speak with a *Smith Manoeuvre Certified Professional* insurance agent who will be able to best tie in all sorts of protection you need with the fact that you will be keeping your mortgage debt level going forward. In any event, you will likely be offered mortgage insurance through the refinance process but mortgage insurance offered by the mortgage lender is seldom a good deal. Very seldom is it a good deal, in fact.

But being properly insured is an important component to successful financial planning that many people overlook. So ask your accredited *Smith Manoeuvre Certified Professional* mortgage broker or investment advisor for a referral to a *Smith Manoeuvre Certified Professional* insurance agent to ensure all your needs are taken care of in the most cost-effective manner. You – and your family – will be glad you did. Take this moment to really look at all aspects of your financial life. A complete and holistic review-slash-reboot.

Other Benefits of Tax Deductions

Let's also look at some of the benefits of *The Smith Manoeuvre* that you may not have thought of up to this point: the incremental benefits enjoyed as regards the effect of your *Smith Manoeuvre* tax deductions on other tax items.

Old Age Security gets clawed back if you make too much – for every dollar of net income over the net income limit, fifteen cents must be 'repaid'. So if your *Smith Manoeuvre* tax deductions bring you under the threshold, you get to keep what otherwise would have been clawed back. Similarly, for medical expenses, your qualified medical expenses for the year must exceed a threshold related to your net income in order to be eligible for the medical expense credit, so as net income decreases, the medical credit enjoyed will increase. Lastly, tax deductions can help increase benefits arising from programs such as the Canada Child Benefit, GST/HST Tax Credit and a number of provincial programs (e.g. childcare, medicines/pharmaceuticals).

The Smith Manoeuvre Homeowner Course

You will have seen me reference this throughout the book, but at this point I would like to formally introduce you to it. *The Smith Manoeuvre Homeowner Course* is a modular online course that expands on many of the concepts in the book and introduces a number of others. There is a great deal of visual aids in the course and much more information on the specifics.

The course was created in part to be able to continuously update any concepts that may need to be 'live' concepts considering the mortgage, tax and investment landscapes are periodically changing, but also, and importantly, to keep the book to a manageable length – after all, who wants to pick up a guide on personal finances that's thicker than a science textbook? Indeed, the amount of content of the in-depth course is greater than this book.

If you decide to proceed with contacting accredited *Smith Manoeuvre Certified Professionals* to assist and advise you in the setup and ongoing implementation of the strategy, having taken the online course will ensure you are as up to date as possible and are able to speak the same language as the professionals you choose to work with. The course will also go into depth on how to use *The Smithman Calculator* and all the various accelerators and options in order for you to be able to calculate your potential results with confidence.

More information on the course can be found at www.smithman.net.

The Smith Manoeuvre Certified Professional Accreditation Program

In your search for a real estate agent, mortgage broker, investment advisor, real estate lawyer/notary, insurance agent or accountant, be sure to ask them if they are accredited as a *Smith Manoeuvre Certified Professional. The Smith Manoeuvre Certified Professional Accreditation Program* was developed to ensure that the professionals assisting Canadians set up, implement and maintain their *Smith Manoeuvre* program have been trained on all aspects of the strategy and have ongoing access to additional resources and a direct line to me here at *The Smith Manoeuvre*, when required.

As mentioned previously, there are a great number of professionals in Canada who don't fully understand all the important aspects of *The Smith Manoeuvre*, whether they think they do or not. *The Smith Manoeuvre* has been around since the mid-80s so certainly there are a great number of professionals who are very well-versed in the strategy and all the nuances it entails from a professional level, but having that accreditation will tell you your financial professionals have gone through the in-depth and comprehensive training.

If the professional you wish to enlist does not have their accreditation, you can have them contact me at smithmanoeuvre.com/info-request as I will need to confirm there are openings in their area considering the number of certifications available for *Smith Manoeuvre Certified Professionals* will be limited.

CHAPTER 8

WHAT'S IN IT FOR THE BANK? OR FOR CANADA?

Life Is Better When the Bank Is Onside

When my dad, Fraser, was first attempting to interest a bank to support his newly-developed strategy, he was turned down by the Royal, the Montreal and the Bank of BC, in that order. "Irregular" was the common reason given for refusing to participate to bring tax relief to Canadian mortgage holders.

Not one to give up, he decided he needed to talk to a bank president. Guessing that he would not be getting an audience anytime soon with the president of CIBC, Fraser elected instead to talk to the head of VanCity Savings. The Chief Executive Officer was Larry Bell, recently arrived from his tenure as Deputy Minister of Finance for British Columbia. Fraser didn't know Larry Bell from a stick, but when he placed his call, the operator put him through without asking his name, and CEO Bell answered the phone himself.

Dad liked him right away. He told Larry he had an idea that would bring VanCity new customers at the expense of the big banks, and he was invited in immediately for a chat.

Larry listened intently to Fraser's story, watched him draw his little pictorial, and when he was finished, Larry pushed his chair back and asked, "Why isn't every Canadian doing this?" And a friendship was born.

What Was It That Interested Larry Bell?

There are several reasons why Larry was interested in *The Smith Manoeuvre* for VanCity's benefit many years ago – and these reasons hold for other banks looking to offer you a readvanceable mortgage so you can implement *The Smith Manoeuvre*.

A) New Customers

Since almost everybody already has a banking relationship, it is a market that is nearly 100% saturated. You may not feel sorry for your bank manager, but he is measured on how many new customers he signs up in the branch each year. As with most businesses, banks need new business to grow, but that's tough to do in the banking business. By offering specialized mortgages which allow the operation of *The Smith Manoeuvre*, they can bring over customers from other banks not offering the appropriate type of mortgage.

B) Collateral Business

The banks love the fact that you moved from one of their competitors over to them. But what really makes them smile is that while they now have a new mortgage customer, they also have a new potential customer for all of their other products – RRSPs, TFSAs, savings accounts, insurance, etc. As we know, the banks are trying to get as much of your 'wallet' as possible, and this gives them an *opportunity* to reach out to you to offer you other investments or services in their portfolio, whether or not you actually take them up on any of their offers.

C) Good Customers

By virtue of the nature of the loan setup that is proposed, the banks can see that the loan risk is very modest. This is partly because the banker's security for the investment lending is the house, not the investments the client will be purchasing. Now considering you will be working with a financial professional in order to make your investment decisions, we can be quite confident that your net worth will be increasing nicely for you over time, but the banker, likely not involved on the investment side of your program, would rather have your house as security for his loan to you. That is what he's used to; that is how it has always been done.

The main reason the loan risk to the bank is so low is because the mortgage lender will not be lending funds to you to invest unless you first reduce the debt on his mortgage. Accordingly, the bank's lending is not increasing the customer's debt; it is simply keeping it at the same level. Up goes the deductible investment loan portion but only after the non-deductible mortgage loan goes down first.

And if the bank really looked hard enough, they'd feel extra comfortable with this arrangement because they would see that with the reborrowing, you are increasing your net worth over time via stable investments rather than harming your net worth due to buying depreciating or disappearing items like cars, groceries or vacations.

D) Self-Maintaining Asset Base

All banks have a built-in problem with their mortgage loan assets. The day you made your first mortgage payment, you reduced your principal a tiny amount in addition to paying a huge amount of non-deductible interest to the bank. While you feel bad about paying all that interest to the bank, the bank feels good because that's how they make their money. While you feel good about paying down your mortgage balance, the bank feels bad, because you have reduced their asset. They start immediately to find other people who need mortgages in order to replace the assets lost each day due to mortgage payments being made across Canada.

However, because *Smith Manoeuvre* clients are reborrowing to invest at the same speed as they were paying off the first mortgage, the consequence is that the bank's asset – your debt – would be maintained at the same level. Because why would you pay off a loan you had just made deductible?

Why indeed!? Your intent should be to die old and wrinkly still owing the mortgage lender that same amount so that you can keep claiming the deductible interest, receiving refunds every year, and enjoying the growth and income from your vast portfolio until you die.

If you complete the conversion and wish to have no debt at all, good or bad, you could elect to divert tax refunds plus former mortgage payments to reduce the deductible loan or use some of your accrued investment assets to make large reductions on the debt, but that is up to you. What the mortgage lender knows is that their asset base is likely to remain for many years to come. And they like that.

The point is that you will have a choice between continuing your investment program or paying off your new tax-deductible loan. This is a luxury many Canadians will not enjoy if they do not avail themselves of at least employing *The Smith Manoeuvre* to convert the debt from the bad kind to the good kind. Convert your debt to the good kind, and then decide whether to keep it or pay it off.

That is the very least even the most debt-averse citizen should entertain. If you already have the debt of a house mortgage, at least convert it from bad debt to good debt. And to be clear, *The Smith Manoeuvre* is reversible. If you wished at any time to redeem the investment assets you have acquired to apply against the line of credit from whence the original funds to invest came, you could certainly do so.

You will be pleased when you decide to utilize *The Smith Manoeuvre*. The financial institutions will also be glad of your decision. But will the tax department be glad you did? Will the Minister of Revenue be excited in a pleasant and positive way when you have engineered all these continuous and very large tax deductions year after year after year? Hmm…

The Tax Department, the Government and the Country

So just where is all this new money coming from that your family is going to receive in order for you to utilize *The Smith Manoeuvre* so that you can:

1. reduce your non-deductible mortgage, so that you can…
2. borrow back your newfound equity the same day, so that you can…
3. buy new investments, so that you can…
4. generate deductible investment loan interest expense, so that you can…
5. claim tax deductions, so that you can…
6. get generous tax refund cheques, so that you can…
7. reduce your non-deductible mortgage, so that you can…
8. borrow back… etc., etc.

It becomes apparent that the tax department is the entity that is going to provide the new money for your family when you engage *The Smith Manoeuvre.*

Let's Use Someone Else's Money for Our Benefit

The Smith Manoeuvre is quite different than other strategies to pay out your mortgage sooner because it generates a new and incremental income for your family via tax deductions, which you are then able to use to pay down your mortgage faster than otherwise possible. In addition, you will have a pool of assets you have purchased with the money you borrowed to invest – all because you received new cash for your family as a result of tax refund cheques that you received from the tax department. This should make you feel better towards the tax department.

Because this investment strategy converts the traditionally non-deductible interest of a house mortgage loan into deductible investment loan interest, the tax department will not be receiving as much tax from you as they have become accustomed to receiving. They will still be collecting a lot from you, but less than usual.

In the narrow confines of the office of the Minister of Revenue, there might be some early consternation at the initial drop in tax revenue because of the refund cheques he will be writing to you when you start using *The Smith Manoeuvre.* Fortunately, the Minister of Revenue, in the longer term, is quite happy to have you using *The Smith Manoeuvre.* The other cabinet ministers are happy about it too.

Deductible Interest – the Lubricant of Business Investment

Most industrialized nations allow the interest expense on business loans to be deducted from the business income of the corporation that does the borrowing. This act reduces the income tax bill of the company. The government understands quite well that it is in their own best interest to provide the tax incentive of tax-deductible interest to businesses making investment decisions for the benefit of their own company. For instance, if the loan interest is deductible, then it makes more palatable the decision to build factories and infrastructure.

The taxman knows that if he does his part to make it easier for the companies to make decisions to borrow to invest in infrastructure, research, marketing and such, there will likely be more profits in the future for the company which the taxman will be able to tax. In addition, the growth of the company will require growth in the number of employed people whom the tax department will be only too happy to tax to the max. This also reduces the number of people on the welfare rolls, reducing government expense in that important area. The people who are working ostensibly spend more providing a stimulus to the economy, further increasing the flows of cash which government also gets to tax to death.

And finally, whereas people who are without work are a strain on the system on a current basis, they are also *not* investors in RRSPs and other investments, which would provide future income for their retirement. The government gains in a large way if the population is employed.

These are some of the reasons that the tax department is happy to allow deductible interest for businesses that borrow to increase their business. And so it should be.

Personal Investing and Tax-Deductible Interest

The wealthier of the population, after the expenses we all have for food, clothing, shelter and income tax, have some money left over at the end of the month to invest. They are also able to afford expensive lawyers and accountants to show them how to take out bank loans for investment purposes and then to deduct their interest on their investment loans, simultaneously. Invest and also reduce income tax at the same time? That's fine by the tax department and is in fact encouraged by the tax department. All wealthy people have done this, are doing it or will do it.

Because the wealthy are able and willing to invest to improve their economic position to even higher levels, they provide the rest of us a service of great benefit. Because of their investment money, new businesses are funded, and the new businesses hire new people. The businesses and the people are taxed, so the taxman is grateful enough to the investor that the taxman will allow the wealthy investor to deduct the interest on any loan he takes out for the purpose of earning more income. The rationale is the same as it is for the first example of the taxman allowing deductions of interest expense for companies.

We Want to Be Investors but We Can't See How

The 90% of the population that are not classified as 'wealthy' are not usually investors. It is not because they don't want to be, it's because they usually find that the cash runs out before the month runs out. How could anyone justify using cash to invest for, say, an 8% return when they are carrying credit card debt at 19.99%? We know that only a minority of Canadians can afford to invest in an RRSP even with its benefits such as tax deductibility of the principal investment plus tax-free compounding. Small wonder that, by far, the bulk of Canadians will come up short of cash flow when the paycheque stops at retirement day.

The Smith Manoeuvre works for almost all Canadians who have a mortgage, whether they are wealthy or not. There is a huge pool of mortgage payers in Canada who are not in the wealthy category. They are working hard to make ends meet, they are getting an education, and they are raising kids. They are also finding it tough to get through many months without employing the credit card.

The tax department will be delighted to find out that *The Smith Manoeuvre* is going to turn this huge group of taxpayers into investors. More investors in Canada means more businesses funded with new money as the mortgages are converted from dead-end home mortgages into productive investment loans.

Lots of Benefits for Canada

The benefits for Canada will be the same as they are from companies that invest, and from wealthy Canadians that invest. And therefore, in the same way the tax department is happy to allow deductions for interest on loans to make income when it applies to business and wealthy investors, they will be happy to allow it for the not-wealthy. If you are in the not-wealthy category, the tax department is standing by to start sending you tax refund cheques if you are wise enough to convert your bad debt to good debt.

Because of the resultant new cash that will begin arriving in the homes of legions of ordinary Canadians derived from these tax refund cheques, these families will be better off themselves. They will have pools of investments instead of dead-end house mortgages, and they will generate lower and lower taxes as they invest more and more. These families will be less likely to need government assistance during their working life or in their retirement.

The tax department is the apparent loser in the short term, but a winner in the longer term. This is why the government, in its wisdom, will continue to bless *The Smith Manoeuvre* and the increase in net worth it will bring to homeowners with mortgages, be they wealthy or not-so-wealthy.

An Imperfect Attempt...

Many years ago, Joe Clark was elected prime minister partly on the strength of his promise to give Canadians tax-deductible mortgages. To his credit, the law was changed and the tax return forms the following year did provide some partial deductions. The Liberals cancelled the program when Joe was defeated at the next election. The flaw in the program was that it was a giveaway. There was no requirement for the homeowner to do any investing/conversion of the mortgage to earn the deductions.

...Greatly Improved

You will receive no tax refunds from the taxman using *The Smith Manoeuvre* unless and until you begin to convert your debt from bad to good by investing for the well-being of yourself, your family, and all Canadians. Investing is good for the people, and therefore it's good for Canada. In the final analysis, this is why the Canada Revenue Agency will be happy to continue to support *The Smith Manoeuvre*, and this is why you will continue to receive tax refunds.

It will sound to some like it is too good to be true, that life is a zero-sum game and therefore it can't possibly be as represented. Classical and modern economists might not agree on the foregoing as it applies to theory, but if you believe in free enterprise and the goodness of capitalism-with-caring, you will understand that we can all be beneficiaries if we enable and encourage this program. *The Smith Manoeuvre* simply extends tax and investment benefits, that have always been in place for business and the wealthy, to the less-wealthy in our society. Surely that will be good for all of us.

CHAPTER 9

SUMMARY – AND WHAT TO DO NEXT

You have learned about *The Smith Manoeuvre*, which is a combination of several different strategies available to you that, once implemented, will improve the financial well-being of your family in dramatic fashion, with very little cost, if any, and no new cash flow required from you on an ongoing basis. It can mean the difference between a retirement of comfort or a retirement of, well…employment.

The Smith Manoeuvre does not require that you increase your debt. Instead you will simply arrange to keep the amount of your existing debt constant for at least the interval of time it takes to *convert* the debt you have now from the bad kind to the good kind. Because debt is not increasing, this is not classified as a leveraging program. It is a debt conversion strategy.

When the conversion process has been completed, you may choose to resume eliminating your debt, even though it is good debt providing you tax refund cheques.

In the alternative, you may decide that you wish to leave the loan in place, paying deductible interest only. In this case you will continue to receive tax refund cheques for the rest of your life, and instead of reducing the loan with your cash flow, you could choose to continue to buy investments for the rest of your life as well. This is typically what wealthy people do as there is no doubt that the growth of net worth is far superior in this latter case. But some will insist on zero debt no matter what it costs to attain it. The decision is yours to make, at your pleasure.

Individual Results Will Vary…

The length of time it will take to convert your existing bad debt to good debt is influenced by several factors. These include your mortgage balance and current rates, family cash flow, the amount of deductible interest you can claim to get tax refunds, and the value of assets you currently own. These current assets might better be liquidated to provide more cash to reduce your non-deductible mortgage loan.

In addition, the efficiency of *The Smith Manoeuvre* can be dramatically improved by diverting existing monthly savings and investment plans against the non-deductible debt. And persons who operate unincorporated businesses or who wish to utilize leveraging strategies can multiply the value of *The Smith Manoeuvre* in dramatic fashion.

As the non-deductible loans are reduced by the foregoing strategies, the identical amount of money is reborrowed to service deductible debt and purchase investment assets. These assets will be free-and-clear because the security for the borrowing will be the house, just as the house was the security for the original non-deductible mortgage loan. If your family were subsequently subjected to a financial disaster, an illness, for example, you could sell off some of your free-and-clear assets to take care of the emergency. The process is reversible.

The Smith Manoeuvre relies on the tax department rules that money borrowed to buy your home, cars, vacations, and consolidation does not generate deductible interest. On the other hand, when you borrow money with the expectation of earning income, the interest expense of that loan *will* be a tax deduction. It is the kind of debt you have that determines its deductibility.

...But You'll Love Yours

You have the debt already. It is bad debt because its interest expense is not tax-deductible. You might as well get it converted to the good kind of debt – deductible debt. You will enjoy receiving those tax refund cheques. They are free (it doesn't cost you anything out of pocket to start earning them) and there is no tax on the proceeds. The conversion from bad debt to good debt is achieved by the purchase of new investments of your choice, one more very large benefit of *The Smith Manoeuvre* for your family.

The Smith Manoeuvre is a legal strategy utilizing standard Canada Revenue Agency tax rules. It is available to any Canadian family with 20% or more equity in their home, or with the ability to engineer 20% or more equity by paying down or borrowing enough from your in-laws to reach that level – borrowing from Peter to pay Paul is not always a bad thing to do.

The Smith Manoeuvre utilizes strategies routinely practiced by businesses and wealthy individuals with the assistance of expensive lawyers and accountants. Finally, via *The Smith Manoeuvre*, ordinary Canadians with ordinary incomes will be able to enjoy these strategies.

To enable you to calculate your personal outcomes if you were to employ *The Smith Manoeuvre* for your family, you will want to order *The Smithman Calculator* at www.smithman.net. This versatile software will show you the results arising from any partial or full implementation of the program. It will allow you to compare 'what-if' variables such as interest rate and growth rate assumption, amortization alterations, and the incremental improvement the various accelerators can offer you.

The Status Quo Is Not Working for Canadians

The financial course currently being travelled by most Canadians these days will yield poor results and broken dreams. Many Canadians are headed for a reverse mortgage, being forced to downsize or work in a big box store or fast food restaurant in their retirement unless they change their strategy of 'first get rid of the mortgage, and only then start to build an investment portfolio'. Adopting *The Smith Manoeuvre* will dramatically improve your chances of optimizing your ability to build significantly more family net worth than you presumed possible thus affording you more pleasant options in retirement and eliminating unpleasant circumstances.

While it is possible for a person with some financial experience to put *The Smith*

Manoeuvre into practice, I recommend you enlist financial professionals to do this work for you. A team consisting of a knowledgeable real estate agent, mortgage broker, investment advisor, real estate lawyer/notary, insurance agent and accountant will be able to tailor your financial situation to your best personal advantage going forward. There are also other circumstances and linkages that good advisors will accommodate on your behalf to ensure no opportunity is missed to optimize the results for your family.

Factors that influence the financial well-being of your family have not been encouraging in Canada in the past few years, and there are few signs that things will get easier for us average Canadians. This means we will have to depend less on government, and more on our own resources. *The Smith Manoeuvre* is remarkably efficient at raising large amounts of real, new wealth for your family while it generates welcome tax refunds.

As well, it causes us to immediately begin building that all-important investment portfolio that will give us peace of mind as it builds, free-and-clear. It is a comfort to live your life knowing you have liquid assets to call upon if the need ever arises.

Make a Change. For You and Your Family. And for Canada

A financially secure Canadian is a financially secure Canada. So join the thousands of Canadians who are already in the process of converting their bad debt to good debt or who have already completed the process. You too can enjoy these financial gains for the benefit of your family, and with these financial gains, you can expect emotional gains – the reduction in stress levels arising from a deeply embedded and constant worrying about the future cannot be underestimated. It is liberating!

I would like to note that somewhere it is written that the two leading causes of relationship breakdown and divorce are issues revolving around sex and money: the two biggest reasons we can't stay together also happen to be two subjects that we learn very little or absolutely nothing about in the school system or in our formative years. Now, I can appreciate the likelihood that some of you may be thinking that you are indeed an expert in one of them already, so start taking care of the other and you will be rewarded with a secure, stable and happy future.

"An investment in knowledge pays the best interest."
- Benjamin Franklin

So What Are Your Next Steps?

1. If you have not already, go to www.smithman.net and order *The Smithman Calculator* to see how the strategy can improve your family's financial condition. This powerful tool allows you to input your own income information, mortgage details, and various assumptions, provides debt consolidation and preservation options, and includes the various powerful accelerators which may be available to you as well as *The Smith Manoeuvre Lite* decelerator. The calculator provides all the information you need in order to make a very important, very valuable decision.

2. You can also find free resources on the website which will help you plan and stay focused and informed. On the website you can sign up for *The Smith Manoeuvre Newsletter* and have access to some simple calculators, PDFs of tax tips and suggestions for scrounging up some extra mortgage prepayment dollars that you won't miss, checklists, suggested readings, and links to other valuable websites. Check back in frequently as the resources will be updated as needed.

3. Let's equate this whole learning process around *The Smith Manoeuvre* to schooling – consider completing this book graduation from *Smithman High School*. Now it's time to go to *Smithman University* – if you would like to take *The Smith Manoeuvre Homeowner Course*, please visit www.smithman.net. This course expands on the content in this book, contains bonus sections on how to strategically borrow money and basic personal finance concepts, helps round out your understanding and provides a video demonstration of *The Smithman Calculator* so you can use it to your best advantage. In this book I talk quite a bit about compound growth. But this concept applies not only to money but to learning as well. The more you learn the faster you grow. In this book I also talk frequently about the differences between the wealthy and the non-wealthy – here's one more: the wealthy view the cost of learning as an investment, the non-wealthy view the cost of learning as an expense.

4. Visit smithmanoeuvre.com/info-request if you are a homeowner and would like us to locate a *Smith Manoeuvre Certified Professional* for you in your area (realtor, mortgage broker, investment advisor, real estate lawyer/notary, insurance agent or accountant). To continue the 'schooling' analogy, these certified professionals have 'post-grad PhD's' in *The Smith Manoeuvre*. And this is very important because

I frequently come across financial professionals who do not fully understand the strategy or have not heard of *The Smith Manoeuvre*. A financial professional has one job – to improve the financial life of their client. And if they don't have a complete understanding or have not heard of *The Smith Manoeuvre* then they may be harming or are not making their clients aware of this potent financial strategy. And if they are not making their clients aware of this strategy then they are withholding information that could increase the net worth of their clients by up to $400,000 or more. So, enlist the services of professionals who have been trained in the strategy and you will get the most out of your *Smith Manoeuvre* and personal finances, and, importantly, you will know that you have found a professional that goes above and beyond.

5. Lastly, share this strategy with your friends and family. Direct them to the website or loan them your copy of the book. This is not some secret you need to keep to yourself – let as many people as possible know that there is help, that there is a better future. If they found out you had the secret to $400,000 or more and didn't tell them, how would they feel? Best not to find out!

So, there you have it, folks. My hope is that you look further into the benefits that *The Smith Manoeuvre* can offer your family, but that even if you don't feel *The Smith Manoeuvre* is for you, then at least you are a little better prepared and knowledgeable about personal finances than before you picked this book up. My hope is that *all* Canadians can be a little better prepared and knowledgeable about personal finances. There are many ways to improve our financial security, not just the strategy discussed in this book, and by making sure we learn all we can we will be better able to steer ourselves away from a future that is full of financial and emotional uncertainty to a future of abundance – not only in terms of wealth, but emotional security and freedom as well.

I'll end off by saying that I'm proud to carry on my father's mission to give every Canadian homeowner the opportunity to say "Yes" to the question, "Do you want to make your mortgage tax-deductible?"

Remember that there are professionals available to help guide you with your *Smith Manoeuvre* and I'm always available for any questions you may have.

Standing by…

Robinson Smith

"Screw it, let's do it!"
- Richard Branson

P.S. ARE YOU A FINANCIAL PROFESSIONAL?

The Smith Manoeuvre strategy can reduce your client's tax bill; have them be rid of their expensive non-deductible mortgage debt in record time, thus saving tens of thousands in non-deductible interest payments; and it can have them building up a significant *Personal Pension Plan* that otherwise would not exist. I firmly believe that a financial professional in Canada cannot deliver the most value to their clients without being fully versed in not only *The Smith Manoeuvre* but, of course, any tax-saving and wealth creation financial strategy.

And if financial professionals are not letting their clients know of financial strategies that can improve their wealth – at least giving them some basic information – then they are relying on someone else to provide them with information that can save them tax or reduce total non-deductible mortgage interest payments or build wealth and security (or accomplish all these goals simultaneously). And isn't assistance and advising on wealth creation and preservation the very job of a financial professional?

But when you show your clients how they can improve their net worth by hundreds of thousands of dollars, they will appreciate your stellar service, will remain loyal to you, and will send their friends and family to you because you will have made it obvious that you are different from your competitors.

For those of your clients that decide this strategy is not for them, at least you were able to demonstrate you are one of the few who provide service levels above and beyond what others in your profession offer. For those clients who want to implement it but aren't quite ready yet, you can help them get into a position where they are ready as quickly as possible.

All that being said, you are obviously a financial professional who cares about providing the best service to your clients considering you are continuing your learning by picking up this book – at least you don't have to worry about having to shake your head when your client asks you, "Have you heard of *The Smith Manoeuvre*?"

If you are a realtor, mortgage broker, investment advisor, real estate lawyer/notary, insurance agent or accountant, and are interested in learning more details about the benefits to your clients and your business by becoming an accredited *Smith Manoeuvre Certified Professional*, which includes territorial exclusivity, please get in touch with me at smithmanoeuvre.com/info-request.

ONE LAST WORD

I would like to end off by reiterating what I allude to a few times in the body of this book. There is a serious lack of financial education opportunities for Canadians. It has been this way since anyone can remember because at no time has there been an inclusive, widespread, systematic, formal education or training program which focuses on explaining the various important aspects of money and personal finance to kids or youth about to enter the workforce.

In my time as an advisor, I met many, many people who had, shall we say, 'misguided' concepts of money. Credit was for taking and money was for spending. Young people with solid prospects and a lot of time to retirement would invest too conservatively, or those towards the more mature end of the age spectrum wanted to go all in on the next big thing. Sometimes the attachment to money was too intense, sometimes there was none at all.

Now, I am not judging these people for their concept of money or credit or investing because I recognize that they probably learned about money and finances from someone other than a financial professional; it is probable they learned from their parents. And where do you think their parents learned about money and finances? That's right – from *their* parents. And what are the chances that someone through the generations of these families were trained financial professionals? Possible but pretty thin. My point is that there is this dangerous chain of knowledge transfer where every subsequent generation is learning from an elder who is not an expert and then passing their imperfect understanding of personal finances down to the next generation and so on. And it must be stopped.

It is nonsensical to think that this is going to produce anything good – it has not so far, and it won't in the future. The chain needs to be broken and kids need to learn about money and finances and credit and the types of debt and budgeting and taxes and, and, and…from someone who actually *is* an expert. We have mathematicians teaching our kids math. We have scientists teaching our kids science. We have engineers teaching our kids engineering. But don't we have financial professionals teaching our kids about finances.

If you have an interest in finances, which it would appear you have if you have read this far, then why not give this book to your son or daughter to read? Or to your sibling's or friends' kids? Maybe they will take an interest or maybe not, but isn't it worth a shot? Share with them other books you read on personal finances. Sit down with them and watch a podcast together. Take them to sit in on a meeting with your financial advisor – tell them you're going for ice cream and a movie if you have to, but get them in the car! Exposing them to something is the first step to generating an interest – granted, it may not go too well; I was a teenager once too! – but why not try?

At least give them an opportunity to take an interest and better the chances of their success and Canada's success. The future of our children and of Canada is too important.

In fact, after doing a little research into the subject of financial education and education in general, what I – and likely you too – have always had an inkling of has been reinforced – the educational system in its entirety is broken. It's not just the fact that our kids aren't being taught about personal finances in school, it's that they are being taught inefficiently on the whole – the whole philosophy of learning and educating needs a rewiring. By transforming the way our youth are taught we can transform the way they learn.

The Smith Manoeuvre is proud to be able to support *Rethink Thinking* because of people like you – the investment that Canadians like you make in your *own* future allows us to support organizations like *Rethink Thinking* in order to invest in our *children's* future. Learn more about this incredible organization, and become involved, as I have, at www.rethinkthinking.ca.

"Too much of what is called 'education' is little more than an expensive isolation from reality."
- Dr. Thomas Sowell

APPENDIX

6th floor - 3795 Carey Rd.
Victoria, BC V8Z 6T8
T. 250.984.6970 | F. 250.984.6988
www.dickson.ca

August 8, 2019

Smith Consulting Group Ltd.
201 - 9800 McDonald Park Rd.
Sidney, BC
V8L 5W5

To whom it may concern:

Review of The Smithman Calculator

We have conducted a review of The Smithman Calculator ("the calculator") located at www.smithman.net with a view to confirming it's basic mathematical assumptions, mechanics of operation, and subsequent results.

The calculator is designed to show the financial effects of converting the non-deductible interest of a mortgage on a principal residence into deductible interest of an equivalent investment loan. This process is commonly referred to as "The Smith Manoeuvre". The calculator generates various outputs which allows the user to see the effects of The Smith Manoeuvre given specific inputs.

Specifically, the calculator displays:

i) the total income required to pay off the mortgage in the absence of The Smith Manoeuvre;
ii) the total tax savings over the term of the mortgage as a result of The Smith Manoeuvre;
iii) the reduction in the term of the mortgage as a result of The Smith Manoeuvre; and
iv) the improvement in the net worth of the individual as a result of The Smith Manoeuvre.

We have checked the assumptions and mechanics of The Smithman Calculator and we confirm that the assumptions are acceptable, and the calculated results are as expected.

Yours very truly,

DICKSON Chartered Professional Accountants
Per:

Francis Rowe
Director
1.250.984.6974
francis@dickson.ca

GLOSSARY

Accelerator(s) - actions which can be taken to speed up the conversion period of the mortgage and increase the rate of investment. Generally, with no new cash required from the homeowner. See the accelerators below:

Debt Swap - swapping non-deductible debt for deductible debt by making a lump sum prepayment against the non-deductible loan portion of the mortgage and reborrowing the same sum to invest. Can be accomplished with cash from savings or redeemed paid-up investments at any time during the conversion process.

Cash Flow Diversion - instead of investing from cash directly on a regular basis, first apply the amount to be invested against the non-deductible loan portion of the mortgage, reborrow the same sum, and then invest. If consolidating or preserving debt at finance or refinance, divert salvaged payments through the mortgage as well.

Cash Flow Dam - apply unincorporated business revenues as a prepayment against the loan portion of the mortgage, then reborrow to service the business expenses. Any excess revenues can be invested in securities to increase your *Personal Pension Plan.*

DRiP - 'Dividend ReInvestment Program'. Instead of having distributions/dividends automatically reinvested, elect to take them in cash and apply as a prepayment against the mortgage, then reborrow the same sum to invest.

Prime the Pump - if any borrowing power exists upon financing or refinancing into a readvanceable mortgage, some or all of this can be invested immediately to boost the tax deductions and growth potential of the portfolio. Consult a financial professional prior to taking on this additional borrowing.

Amortization - a period in which a debt is reduced or paid off by regular payments.

Balance Transfer - transfer an existing balance on one side of the readvanceable mortgage to the other side. Generally executed in order to either a) attain a zero balance on the line of credit/investment loan portion of the mortgage in order to isolate non-deductible and deductible debt going forward during the conversion process, or, b) isolate newly non-deductible debt from existing deductible debt in order to maintain purity of deductibility of the investment loan going forward.

Canada Savings Bond (CSB) - a Canada Savings Bond is a financial product issued by the Bank of Canada, inspired by war bonds issued during World War I.

Compound Growth - compound growth is the rate of return that represents the cumulative effect that a series of gains has on an amount of capital over time.

Canada Pension Plan (CPP) - the Canada Pension Plan is one of three levels of Canada's retirement income system, which is responsible for paying retirement or disability benefits.

Conversion Process - the process of converting the non-deductible debt of a home mortgage loan to the deductible debt of an investment loan. The amount of time this conversion takes is dependent on a number of factors including your mortgage balance and terms and the number of accelerators available to you.

Corporation - a company or group of people authorized to act as a single entity (legally a person) and recognized as such in law.

Deductible - able to be deducted, especially from taxable income or tax to be paid.

Defined Benefit Pension Plan (DB) - a company pension plan in which an employee's pension payments are calculated according to length of service and the salary they earned at the time of retirement.

Defined Contribution Pension Plan (DC) - a defined contribution plan is a type of retirement plan in which the employer, employee or both make contributions on a regular basis. In defined contribution plans, future benefits fluctuate on the basis of investment earnings.

Down Payment - an initial payment made when something is bought on credit.

Guaranteed Investment Certificate (GIC) - a guaranteed investment certificate is a deposit investment security that Canadian banks and trust companies sell.

High-Ratio Mortgage - a high-ratio mortgage is a mortgage in which a borrower places a down payment of less than 20% of the purchase price on a home. Another way of phrasing a high-ratio mortgage is one with a loan to value ratio of more than 80%. A mortgage with more than a 20% down payment is called a conventional mortgage.

Leverage - use of borrowed capital for an investment, expecting the profits made to be greater than the interest payable; or, use (something) to maximum advantage.

Loan-to-Value (LTV) - the LTV is the ratio between the loan's size and the dollar value of the property. The maximum loan-to-value ratio is the largest allowable ratio of a loan's size to the dollar value of the property.

Marginal Tax Rate (MTR) - a marginal tax rate is the amount of tax paid on an additional dollar of income.

Mortgage Term - a mortgage term is the length of time, usually in years (generally five), in which the parameters of a mortgage have legal effect. After the expiration of the mortgage term, the remaining balance of the mortgage will need to be renewed, refinanced or paid in full.

Non-registered Account - non-registered accounts are a type of investment account used by Canadian citizens which are not registered with the government.

Old Age Security (OAS) - the Old Age Security (OAS) program is the Government of Canada's largest pension program. It is funded out of the general tax revenues of the Government of Canada. The OAS pension is a monthly payment available to seniors aged 65 and older who meet the Canadian legal status and residence requirements.

Open Account - see "non-registered account".

Personal Chequing Account - in the context of *The Smith Manoeuvre*, this is the bank account that you likely already have which services your existing mortgage payments.

Personal Pension Plan - an investment portfolio which can provide retirement cash flow, comfort and security. As it is non-registered, there are no restrictions on how you enjoy it – no mandatory withdrawals or minimums or age requirements.

Proprietorship - a business or property, etc., owned by a proprietor. Not a corporation.

Readvanceable Mortgage - a mortgage with two or more lending facilities – an amortizing loan portion plus at least one other line, typically a line of credit but could be amortizing, which allows the homeowner to reborrow any equity created by the regular mortgage payment (and any prepayments) in order to theoretically always have an outstanding balance equal to the original total loan of the mortgage.

Real Estate Investment Trust (REIT) - a real estate investment trust, or REIT, is a company that owns, operates or finances income-producing real estate.

Red Truck IPA - possibly the best beer around.

Registered Retirement Savings Plan (RRSP) - a Registered Retirement Savings Plan (RRSP) is a retirement savings and investing vehicle for employees and the self-employed in Canada.

Reverse Mortgage - a financial agreement in which a homeowner relinquishes equity in their home in exchange for a lump sum or regular payments, typically to supplement retirement income.

Sequential Approach (The) - the common approach to two of life's most pressing financial demands. Typically, people focus on paying down the mortgage before starting to save for retirement. This results in foregoing the advantage of compound growth.

Smith Manoeuvre Certified Professional Accreditation Program (The) - accreditation program and examination for financial professionals involved in helping guide Canadian homeowners through the initiation, set up and ongoing maintenance of *The Smith Manoeuvre*. The course is designed for real estate agents, mortgage brokers, financial planners, real estate lawyers/notaries, insurance agents and accountants.

Smith Manoeuvre Chequing Account - a dedicated chequing account linked to the line of credit/investment loan component of the readvanceable mortgage to be used exclusively for investment or servicing of deductible investment loan interest.

Smith Manoeuvre Homeowner Course (The) - modular course designed to give the Canadian homeowner a more complete and rounded understanding of *The Smith Manoeuvre* including more specifics on appropriate mortgage financing and functionality, common mistakes, current regulations in the areas of mortgage and taxation, video demonstration of *The Smithman Calculator* and other important up-to-date information. Bonus sections on How to Effectively Borrow Money and a Guide to Basic Personal Finances in Canada to ensure a solid financial foundation.

Tax-Free Savings Account (TFSA) - the Tax-Free Savings Account (TFSA) is an account that does not apply taxes on any interest earned, dividends, or capital gains, and can be withdrawn tax-free.

Tax Refund - a tax refund is a refund on taxes paid to an individual or household when the actual tax liability is less than the amount paid.

Tax Return - a form on which a taxpayer makes an annual statement of income and personal circumstances, used by the tax authorities to assess liability for tax.

ABOUT THE AUTHOR

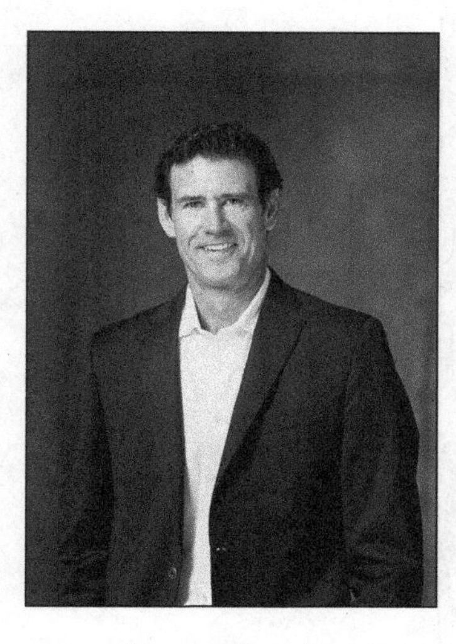

Robinson graduated from the University of Victoria with a double major in Economics and Chinese Studies in 1995. During his time at UVic, he also studied Mandarin in Beijing and Shanghai and upon graduation worked in various sectors in China including international trade and investment while serving as acting Commercial Counselor at the Canadian Embassy in Beijing.

After obtaining an International Business MBA from Simon Fraser University in 2003, Robinson returned again to China to become vice president of The Balloch Group, a boutique international investment bank based in Beijing, and worked on various projects as diverse as seaports, steel cable manufacture, lumber joint ventures and hydrogen fuel-cell investment. He has dined and mingled with the likes of Henry Kissinger, Prime Minister Jean Chretien and the Premier of China, yet somehow still manages to maintain an air of superiority.

In 2006, Robinson returned to Victoria to work with his father, Fraser – the financial strategist who pioneered *The Smith Manoeuvre* – where Robinson helped over 500 families implement the strategy one at a time. In 2018, Robinson sold his investment advisory practice in order to write *Master Your Mortgage for Financial Freedom*, the follow-up to his father's original book, and reach even more Canadians.

Robinson now dedicates his time writing, speaking and training both homeowners and financial professionals in *The Smith Manoeuvre* strategy in order to continue on with his father's original mission to give every Canadian homeowner the opportunity to say "Yes" to the question, "Do you want to make your mortgage tax-deductible?"

He lives in Victoria, BC, with his wife, Heidi, and their dog, Harley.

ABOUT THE ILLUSTRATOR

Emily is an aspiring 14-year-old entrepreneur and artist who began detailed drawings at a very young age.

She started her first paper route at the age of nine and quickly understood the importance of service, connection, and contribution. Realizing her delivery route would provide her the opportunity to spread joy through her love of art, she began delivering custom-designed holiday-themed works of art with her newspapers. Her newspaper clients continue to tell her they look forward to her next piece.

Emily is honoured and grateful to her Uncle Rob for providing her the opportunity to bring some artistic flair to an incredibly boring subject.

Emily lives on Vancouver Island with her sister, Ava, her dad, Eric, and her beautiful and charming mother, Jen, who is much smarter than Emily's Uncle Rob even though she hasn't yet written a book.

Umm…Emily, did you write your bio…or your mom? – Uncle Rob

ROBINSON'S UPCOMING BOOK

Robinson is currently hard at work on his new book surrounding the psychology of money. It will explain why we think, feel or react the way we do in circumstances involving spending, saving or investing money. The seeds of this new book were planted early on in his career as an investment advisor as he witnessed a huge variety of behaviours and thought patterns from his clients. Reactions as diverse as loading up on as much credit as the banks would allow to foregoing simple, affordable and reasonable purchases due to a fear of never having enough. Following is an excerpt:

I have many years of professional experience surrounding money. I have spent a lot of time around a lot of money. Before I turned to writing and speaking in the hopes of getting out to more than just one family at a time, I was a licensed investment advisor with over 500 families as clients. I managed their money. But what interested me was not the actual management of the money. What interested me was the management of the people.

It interested me because it terrified me.

Just one example – near the beginning of my career, I was interviewing a potential client and reviewing his finances. Prepared to react empathetically, I asked him why his outstanding credit card balance of $30,000 matched the total limit of his credit cards exactly. To the penny. Expecting to hear the usual, "Life is expensive and I have no money at the end of the month to make anything other than the minimum payment required," his answer shocked me: "With all these banks willing to give me money, I'd be an idiot not to take it."

"With all these banks willing to *give* me money..."

That $30,000 balance was probably costing him around $1,000 per month just for the privilege of continuing to owe someone else money – but at least he wasn't being an idiot...

I've thought about and told that story many times over the years. I have often wondered what money was to this man. What was this man's relationship with money? Was money his friend? His enemy? His lover? A simple acquaintance? Now, that may sound like a strange question to ask, but do not kid yourself – everyone has a relationship with money.

You have a relationship with money.

And your relationship with money – the way you view it, feel about it, shy away from it or run to it – has affected your finances to date, and will continue to affect your finances going forward. To the good or to the bad, you don't really know right now unless you are one of the very few who have taken a good, hard look. And then only if you knew what you were looking for.

Chances are high that even if you did have a good, hard think about money and what it is to you, you'd likely be pfaffing around in the dark because it is so difficult to be objective about money. Personal finance is one of the few things we are not formally taught in school, and so the patterns we develop around the subject are formed by watching others – typically our parents, sometimes our friends – and they are so deeply ingrained at a young age, and largely on our own, that we don't question our beliefs or behaviours. They are part of us. Did your dad used to come home quite often with a brand-new car? Do you? Did your mom price comparison shop when she took you to the grocery store or did she simply throw items in the cart without looking at the cost? Do you shop the same way?

Only when we understand why we do what we do with money, or don't do, only when we can put a name to our behaviours can we start to make the changes we need to in order to provide more stability and security for our families. Just as in medicine, we can't treat before we diagnose. We need to know what it is we're dealing with before we can prescribe a solution.